# The Lord of the Rings, Vols. 1–3

# 33 1/3 Global

**33 1/3 Global**, a series related to but independent from **33 1/3**, takes the format of the original series of short, music-based books and brings the focus to music throughout the world. With initial volumes focusing on Japanese and Brazilian music, the series will also include volumes on the popular music of Australia/Oceania, Europe, Africa, the Middle East, and more.

### 33 1/3 Japan

Series Editor: Noriko Manabe

Spanning a range of artists and genres—from the 1970s rock of Happy End to technopop band Yellow Magic Orchestra, the Shibuya-kei of Cornelius, classic anime series *Cowboy Bebop*, J-Pop/EDM hybrid Perfume, and vocaloid star Hatsune Miku—**33 1/3 Japan** is a series devoted to in-depth examination of Japanese popular music of the twentieth and twenty-first centuries.

### Published Titles:

Supercell's *Supercell* by Keisuke Yamada

*AKB48* by Patrick W. Galbraith and Jason G. Karlin

Yoko Kanno's *Cowboy Bebop Soundtrack* by Rose Bridges

Perfume's *Game* by Patrick St. Michel

Cornelius's *Fantasma* by Martin Roberts

Joe Hisaishi's *My Neighbor Totoro: Soundtrack* by Kunio Hara

Shonen Knife's *Happy Hour* by Brooke McCorkle

Nenes' *Koza Dabasa* by Henry Johnson

Yuming's *The 14th Moon* by Lasse Lehtonen

Toshiko Akiyoshi-Lew Tabackin Big Band's *Kogun* by E. Taylor Atkins

### Forthcoming Titles:

Yellow Magic Orchestra's *Yellow Magic Orchestra* by Toshiyuki Ohwada

Kohaku utagassen: The Red and White Song Contest by Shelley Brunt

S.O.B.'s *Don't Be Swindle* by Mahon Murphy and Ran Zwigenberg

**33 1/3 Brazil**

Series Editor: Jason Stanyek

Covering the genres of samba, tropicália, rock, hip hop, forró, bossa nova, heavy metal and funk, among others, **33 1/3 Brazil** is a series devoted to in-depth examination of the most important Brazilian albums of the twentieth and twenty-first centuries.

**Published Titles:**

Caetano Veloso's *A Foreign Sound* by Barbara Browning

Tim Maia's *Tim Maia Racional Vols. 1 &2* by Allen Thayer

João Gilberto and Stan Getz's *Getz/Gilberto* by Brian McCann

Gilberto Gil's *Refazenda* by Marc A. Hertzman

Dona Ivone Lara's *Sorriso Negro* by Mila Burns

Milton Nascimento and Lô Borges's *The Corner Club* by Jonathon Grasse

Racionais MCs' *Sobrevivendo no Inferno* by Derek Pardue

Naná Vasconcelos's *Saudades* by Daniel B. Sharp

Chico Buarque's First *Chico Buarque* by Charles A. Perrone

**Forthcoming titles:**

Jorge Ben Jor's *África Brasil* by Frederick J. Moehn

**33 1/3 Europe**

Series Editor: Fabian Holt

Spanning a range of artists and genres, **33 1/3 Europe** offers engaging accounts of popular and culturally significant albums of Continental Europe and the North Atlantic from the twentieth and twenty-first centuries.

**Published Titles:**

Darkthrone's *A Blaze in the Northern Sky* by Ross Hagen

Ivo Papazov's *Balkanology* by Carol Silverman

Heiner Müller and Heiner Goebbels's *Wolokolamsker Chaussee* by Philip V. Bohlman

Modeselektor's *Happy Birthday!* by Sean Nye

Mercyful Fate's *Don't Break the Oath* by Henrik Marstal

Bea Playa's *I'll Be Your Plaything* by Anna Szemere and András Rónai

Various Artists' *DJs do Guetto* by Richard Elliott

Czesław Niemen's *Niemen Enigmatic* by Ewa Mazierska and Mariusz Gradowski

Massada's *Astaganaga* by Lutgard Mutsaers

Los Rodriguez's *Sin Documentos* by Fernán del Val and Héctor Fouce

Édith Piaf's *Récital 1961* by David Looseley

Nuovo Canzoniere Italiano's *Bella Ciao* by Jacopo Tomatis

Iannis Xenakis's *Persepolis* by Aram Yardumian

Vopli Vidopliassova's *Tantsi* by Maria Sonevytsky

Amália Rodrigues's *Amália at the Olympia* by Lila Ellen Gray

Ardit Gjebrea's *Projekt Jon* by Nicholas Tochka

Aqua's *Aquarium* by C.C. McKee

Einstürzende Neubauten's *Kollaps* by Melle Jan Kromhout and Jan Nieuwenhuis

J.M.K.E.'s *To the Cold Land* by Brigitta Davidjants

**Forthcoming Titles:**

Taco Hemingway's *Jarmark* by Kamila Rymajdo

Tripes' *Kefali Gemato Hrisafi* by Dafni Tragaki

Silly's *Februar* by Michael Rauhut

CCCP's *Fedeli Alla Linea's 1964-1985 Affinità-Divergenze Fra Il Compagno Togliatti E Noi Del Conseguimento Della Maggiore Età* by Giacomo Bottà

**33 1/3 Oceania**

Series Editors: Jon Stratton (senior editor) and Jon Dale (specializing in books on albums from Aotearoa/New Zealand)

Spanning a range of artists and genres from Australian Indigenous artists to Maori and Pasifika artists, from Aotearoa/New Zealand noise music to Australian rock, and including music from Papua and other Pacific islands, **33 1/3 Oceania** offers exciting accounts of albums that illustrate the wide range of music made in the Oceania region.

**Published Titles:**

John Farnham's *Whispering Jack* by Graeme Turner

The Church's *Starfish* by Chris Gibson

Regurgitator's *Unit* by Lachlan Goold and Lauren Istvandity

Kylie Minogue's *Kylie* by Adrian Renzo and Liz Giuffre

Alastair Riddell's *Space Waltz* by Ian Chapman

Hunters & Collectors's *Human Frailty* by Jon Stratton

The Front Lawn's *Songs from the Front Lawn* by Matthew Bannister

Bic Runga's *Drive* by Henry Johnson

The Dead C's *Clyma est mort* by Darren Jorgensen

Ed Kuepper's *Honey Steel's Gold* by John Encarnacao

Chain's *Toward the Blues* by Peter Beilharz

Hilltop Hoods' *The Calling* by Dianne Rodger

Screamfeeder's *Kitten Licks* by Ben Green and Ian Rogers

Soundtrack from *Saturday Night Fever* by Clinton Walker

The Avalanches' *Since I Left You* by Charles Fairchild

The Clean's *Boodle Boodle Boodle* by Geoff Stahl

John Sangster's *The Lord of the Rings, Vols. 1–3* by Bruce Johnson

**Forthcoming Titles:**

The Triffids' *Born Sandy Devotional* by Christina Ballico

Crowded House's *Together Alone* by Barnaby Smith

5MMM's *Compilation Album of Adelaide Bands 1980* by Collette Snowden

INXS' *Kick* by Ryan Daniel and Lauren Moxey

Sunnyboys' *Sunnyboys* by Stephen Bruel

Eyeliner's *Buy Now* by Michael Brown

Silverchair's *Frogstomp* by Jay Daniel Thompson

TISMs *Machiavelli and the Four Seasons* by Tyler Jenke

The La De Das' *The Happy Prince* by John Tebbutt

Gary Shearston's *Dingo* by Peter Mills

**33 1/3 South Asia**

Series Editor: Natalie Sarrazin

From the films of Bollywood and Lollywood, to home-grown *bhangra* hip-hop, Hindu devotional pop and Sufi rock, Sri Lankan rap, Indo jazz and disco, new-wave electronica and diasporic Asian Underground scene, **33 1/3 South Asia** takes readers on a sonically diverse journey through the most significant soundtracks and albums from the twentieth and twenty-first centuries.

**Published:**

*Dil Chahta Hai* Soundtrack by Jayson Beaster-Jones

Lata Mangeshkar's *My Favourites, Volume 2* by Anirudha Bhattacharjee and Chandrashekhar Rao

**Forthcoming:**

*Coke Studio* (Season 14) by Rakae Rehman Jamil and Khadija Muzaffar

# The Lord of the Rings, Vols. 1–3

Bruce Johnson

Series Editors: Jon Stratton, UniSA Creative, University of South Australia, and Jon Dale, University of Melbourne, Australia

BLOOMSBURY ACADEMIC
NEW YORK · LONDON · OXFORD · NEW DELHI · SYDNEY

BLOOMSBURY ACADEMIC
Bloomsbury Publishing Inc
1385 Broadway, New York, NY 10018, USA
50 Bedford Square, London, WC1B 3DP, UK
29 Earlsfort Terrace, Dublin 2, Ireland

BLOOMSBURY, BLOOMSBURY ACADEMIC and the Diana logo are
trademarks of Bloomsbury Publishing Plc

First published in the United States of America 2025



A catalog record for this book is available from the Library of Congress.

ISBN: HB: 979-8-7651-2111-5
PB: 979-8-7651-2112-2
ePDF: 979-8-7651-2114-6
eBook: 979-8-7651-2113-9

Typeset by Deanta Global Publishing Services, Chennai, India
Printed and bound in Great Britain

Series: 33 1/3 Oceania

To find out more about our authors and books visit www.bloomsbury.com
and sign up for our newsletters.

# Contents


Acknowledgements  x

Introduction  1

## Part I

**1    Sangster: The times**  11

**2    Sangster: The life**  35

## Part II

**3    Sangster: The sensibility**  61

**4    Sangster: The aesthetics, *The Lord of the Rings***  77

References  113
Index  118

# Acknowledgements

Award-winning pianist Timothy Stevens is in the first rank among Australia's rising generation of jazz musicians. What is less generally known is that he is also one of our leading historians of Australian jazz, and in particular, of the late John Sangster, the creative mind behind the subject of this monograph. Without Timothy's knowledge and his unconditional generosity in giving access to his own unsurpassed archives on Sangster, I could not have written this volume, which may be regarded as a 'teaser' for the Sangster biography that I very much hope Timothy will one day undertake. I thank him for his unstinting advice and assistance in the preparation of this study, and, in particular, for his detailed timeline of Sangster's life and career.

This is also an appropriate moment to pay tribute to Melbourne-based jazz archivist Roger Beilby. Roger pioneered Australian jazz archiving, and as long as around nearly half a century ago, he gave me unrestricted access to his private collection. His hand is apparent throughout the following study, though not always explicitly attributable.

My thanks also to the series editor Jon Stratton for enlarging the remit of this series to allow me to discuss not just a single album, which is the norm for this series, but an entire *oeuvre* unified under the rubric of Tolkien's *Lord of the Rings*, and for bearing with the distinctive format and structure that encompassing a minimum of six albums entails.

As so often in my publications, I want to thank my friend and colleague Liz Giuffre, who has again brought to bear her skills to the final formatting of the MS.

More broadly, I would like to express my continuing gratitude to the community of musicians with whom I have worked over some six decades, many of whom are represented on the recordings studied here. Apart from the pleasure of making music with them, they have in many informal ways, such as gig chats (for many of which they have requested anonymity), opened up many lines of enquiry which have led to this study. My thanks to you all.

# Introduction

My first personal encounter with John Sangster was at a party at the house of jazz archivist Bill Haesler in Balmain, around 1972. Born and raised in Adelaide, where I began my career as a jazz musician, I had recently arrived in Sydney after a couple of years in the UK, mainly London. The guests at the party included a number of ex-Melbourne jazz musicians with whom I had played in my Adelaide days, and there were the jam sessions that were inevitable in such company. Also present was a jovial guest wearing a weird headdress that was like a jester's cap, with baubles and plastic ping-pong-sized balls attached by coiled springs. I think they even lit up from time to time, the whole providing a jolly theatrical diversion as its owner played a washboard. I knew him by name – another ex-Melbournian – and had heard him play very hot trumpet with the Ray Price Quartet in The Velvet Tavern jazz venue during their visit to Adelaide in the 1960s. Much later, in the late 1970s and resident in Sydney, I became a member of the Price band, but on that earlier occasion, over-awed by their celebrity, I had not spoken to any of the members of the Quartet: Price on banjo, Pat Rose on clarinet, Col Nolan on piano and John Sangster on trumpet. And now here he was, the colourful Hobbit-like, washboard-playing centre of a Balmain jazz party. The Sangster/Hobbit persona was successfully cultivated and widely accepted, as recorded by Andrew Bisset: 'There is an unmistakable resemblance between Sangster and the stout Hobbit who is fond of simple jests, eating, drinking, and good company. Sangster combined musicians from different jazz backgrounds on pieces which range from jovially traditional to atmospherically modern. He likes to call it "cosmic Dixieland"' (Bisset 1987: 166).

But I was to discover a very different Sangster in our next direct encounter, which was on a gig. I was a member of Dick Hughes' band, hired to play at a private party at an ostentatiously opulent residence on the north shore, and, as I recall, Sangster was present as a supplementary member or special guest. It was the first time we had met as far as he was concerned. He was a delight to play with. He possessed what I think is the single most important virtue for a collectively improvising musician: he listened. He conducted a musical conversation rather than a self-absorbed monologue. Between sets, he asked me where I had come from – I told him that I had played in Adelaide, in the same venue I had heard him with Ray Price. He was irresistibly charming and made some very complimentary comments to me about my own playing and suggested that now I was living in Sydney, we might do some work together. All this was deeply flattering for this young new arrival in the Big City, and coming from a legendary muso.

As we talked, he surveyed the décor of the room, which he seemed to find in some way objectionably lush, fastidious and 'over-arranged'. He then asked me to join him in some covert destructive prank at the expense of the owners. I can't now recall exactly what it was – but I think it involved raiding the opulent drinks cabinet and stealing a bottle of expensive spirits which we could then share. It struck me at the time as having a class dimension, a bit of malicious *épater le bourgeois*. This was consistent with other aspects of Sangster's personality, as exemplified below in relation to Pat Rose, and with a comment made by his musical colleague Tony Gould, who recalled that 'the main reason we go to the early opener pub before the recording studio is that he mingles with the wharfies who have just come off the job. And we stand among them and he is genuinely interested in their talk' (cited Williams 1981: 71).

In any event, on receiving his invitation to join him in some mischief I declined, saying something to the effect that I wasn't drinking on the gig, and that 'No, we've been hired by these people to play music for them, and that's what I am going to do'. The change in his whole manner towards me was deeply and unforgettably disturbing. Two counts against me: no drinking and no mischief. I recall the abrupt disappearance of the twinkle in his eyes, replaced by a volcanic look at the idea of my not going meekly along with his prank. Although I often heard him play subsequently, we never worked together again. As I was to discover, as with other musicians with whom he had some kind of falling-out, he 'locked me out'.[1]

----

[1] In something of a puzzled aside: In his autobiography *Seeing the Rafters*, he referred to me, not by name, but as someone who had written articles about the El Rocco jazz venue, which he dismissed as uninformed because I was a newly arrived 'pommy pedant' (Sangster 1988: 134) – clearly, he knew my name. But he also inscribed my copy of his book in a genial, matey fashion: 'For Bruce – keep sealed whilst playing your cornet.

Thus to avoid the
dreaded trumpeter's nemesis – the
Farmer Giles
Best love –
Sango.
(John Sangster)'

At the private party on the North Shore, the genial Hobbit suddenly turned into a vicious Orc. Sangster the prankster had turned from light to dark. But, as this brief monograph seeks to argue, these two poles bracketed the prolific work of someone I admire as the most emotionally and stylistically wide-ranging jazz-based musician/composer that this country has ever produced. And nowhere is this protean range more dramatically demonstrated than in his epic *Lord of the Rings* project.

This study thus departs from the usual pattern of the series in that its focus is not on a single recording, but on a cohesive multi-album *oeuvre*, based on the books by J. R. R. Tolkien (1892–1973). This was decades before the cycle became internationally familiar through the films of Peter Jackson from 2001 to 2003. In the 1970s Tolkien's work was relatively obscure, ardently admired by a very small coterie. That is, Sangster was not 'cashing in' on a vogue, but was mining a largely unknown seam dear to his heart. The total project produced three double LP volumes (in 1974, 1976 and 1977), and if we add the 'overture', *The Hobbit Suite*, and the 'coda', *Landscapes of Middle Earth* in 1978 (though I won't include them in detail in this study), it comes to around ninety pieces of music, running to over eight hours.

To explicate the importance and scope of this 'magnum opus', it is impractical and uninstructive simply to run through each LP with a track-by-track synopsis, summarizing what the



---

Then in 1988 I taped a lengthy interview with him at his home in Narrabeen for the Australia Council Research Centre. Yet on none of these occasions did he show any signs of connecting all these events with the same person, me.

reader can hear for themselves by listening to the recordings. Instead, I want to encompass a broader horizon, providing an overview of the music that situates it in the larger cultural landscape out of which it emerged. In doing so, this will also throw light on one of the most extraordinary chapters in the history of the arts in Australia: the wave of creativity that washed out of Melbourne in the years following the Second World War, in which Sangster was nurtured.

Thus, following this introduction, I wish to make a survey of the historical context: John Sangster – the Times. What were the circumstances from which he emerged? This will embrace a wide-ranging cultural and artistic landscape unlike any other in post-settler Australia, at least to that time. To a large extent, it was the product of the Second World War, which gave momentum to the arts in Melbourne in two significant ways. The wartime mobilization of young Australian service personnel revealed and therefore contributed to the existence of an interstate community of like-minded jazz enthusiasts. And these young men (it was a very blokey community) had been brought to a high level of independent mindedness by the interruption of the usual peacetime and relatively uneventful growth to manhood, their maturation accelerated by wartime service. They entered their post-war peacetime careers with sensibilities developed to a higher degree than would have been the case in more pacific times. In the particular case of Melbourne, the second most populated metropolis in Australia, these independent spirits stood out in sharp relief against a generally conservative background. They constituted a progressive movement that expressed itself in literature, painting and music, all in consort, and manifested itself in the establishment of what is now the world's longest-running annual jazz festival. This was the Australian Jazz Convention, inaugurated in 1946, and through which John Sangster made his national public debut.

In the subsequent chapter, we survey John Sangster – the Life. The relationship between the artist and the art is a matter of perennial debate. In this instance, I take the position that the two are inextricable, particularly given that he described his *Lord of the Rings* suite as his musical autobiography. In the words of Andrew Bisset, what distinguishes jazz musicians is 'they are what they play and they play what they are' (Bisset 1987: 127). The magnitude of his achievement, its emotional complexity and stylistic range unmatched in Australian music, is, I believe, best appreciated not by separating the man from his art, but by seeing them as symbiotic. Sangster the artist is indivisible from Sangster the man. The man himself and his actions were a bewildering enigma running the full spectrum from light to darkness, from Hobbit to Orc. An overview of that life illuminates the wellsprings of his most monumental *oeuvre*, *The Lord of the Rings* and its framing projects.

This takes us to John Sangster and his music. *The Lord of the Rings* suite runs to around eight hours of music, far too massive to be able to investigate every song in detail. What I therefore seek to do is to embed descriptive analyses of the pieces within, and exemplifying, the larger context of his sensibility and aesthetics. These will illustrate the massive scope of the project along several axes. It encompasses an emotional range from whimsical geniality to the 'heart of darkness'. At the same time, it runs the formal gamut from traditional jazz styles to the most avant-garde, from the exquisitely sculpted to free-form aleatory, from music to noise. It embodies almost the totality of the history of jazz, even drawing upon aspects and the instrumentation of chamber music.

The second major section thus seeks to extrapolate from both his music and his own words the artistic sensibility that produced and sustained his work. This enterprise is, on the face of it, impeded by his own carefully crafted Ocker persona, as presented particularly in his autobiography *Seeing the Rafters*. The book is written in an effervescent vernacular that would be incomprehensible outside Australia, and even to many Australians; it is in many ways a private language for the freemasonry of the musicians with whom he generally worked. It avoids anything resembling a serious artistic statement, yet this itself is a form of manifesto. Taken in conjunction with an account of what we know of his working methods, on stage and particularly in the recording studio, we can assemble a picture of the aesthetic that generated the compositional output of a man who sought to deflect any sense that he had any aesthetic other than to have fun.

This section, I suggest, points to the need for a full biography of Sangster, beyond doubt one of our most creative composers, as well as most prolific. Apart from the 250 or so songs he recorded listed under his own name in Mitchell's first Australian jazz discography covering the years 1925–80, most of them his own compositions, and all the tracks he recorded with other groups, and those listed in the later Mitchell discographies, there is a listing of a further compositional body of unrecorded work of around fifty items from 1993 to his death in 1995 (Mitchell 1988; Mitchell 1998, Mitchell 2002. The unpublished list, headed 'John Sangster Unrecorded Brisbane

Works 1993-1995', was kindly provided to me by Timothy Stevens[2]). A fully dedicated biography is needed.

Finally, I want to emphasize that everything in the following is, or has been permitted to be, a matter of public record. These include published records, and anyone with the smallest particle of curiosity could discover the information with a Google click, such as Trove for contemporary press coverage. Or, with a slightly stronger research purpose, by referring to documents for general inspection in public institutions like the Mitchell Library. Where an oral source has requested that certain information not be used, or if used, not attributed, in every case this has been respected. There are no confidences betrayed here. To furtively omit information that does not just preserve a mythology simply makes the historian, and the scholarly field they represent, look naïve, unreliable and immature. Australian jazz scholarship is now more grown-up than that.



---

[2] Mitchell 1988; Mitchell 1998; Mitchell 2002. The unpublished list, headed 'John Sangster Unrecorded Brisbane Works 1993-1995', courtesy Timothy Stevens.

# PART I

# 1 Sangster
## The times

John Sangster became involved as a tyro on the Melbourne jazz scene at a particularly propitious moment. As his slightly younger contemporary, pianist Dick Hughes (b. 1931), recalled in his memoir, in the year he did his Leaving Certificate, 'Something new and exciting was happening on the Melbourne jazz scene in 1946' (Hughes 1977: 6).[1]

That 'something new and exciting' was the outcome of an array of circumstances, local, national and international. Hughes is describing an ethos that to a large extent was created by the Second World War, 1939–45. Wartime mobilizations had thrown together a cohort of young people from across the continent who would otherwise never have met, and this aggregation included fellow enthusiasts for what has become known as the 'classic' jazz tradition. Opportunities were created by wartime postings to interact with other jazz fans and musicians. In doing so, they began to gain a random glimpse of the national scope of jazz interest, the sense that there might be a national 'community', as for example at a servicemen's jazz club formed in Port Moresby (Sandford

---

[1]There is a photograph of a young Dick Hughes on a truck with other attendees, including Sangster, at the second Australian Jazz Convention, in Johnson 1987: 89.

2018: 42–4). Some of these contacts were also with visiting US service musicians, such as Black trumpet player Maurice Goode, whose photograph with fellow trumpet player Roger Bell would adorn the printed programme for the first Australian Jazz Convention in 1946, of which more below (Johnson 2023A: 8). Encounters with US musicians also included members of the visiting Artie Shaw's orchestra. Although the Shaw concerts were only for US military personnel, by various subterfuges, locals also often managed to attend or overhear these concerts and mingle with orchestra members, and, in the case of the Roger Bell band, this led to a recording with one of the orchestra's trumpet players, Max Kaminsky (Bell 1988: 45–50; Mitchell 1988: 47).

The demobilization at war's end in 1945 also saw the re-entry into the civilian populace of a cohort of young people who had experienced up to six years of maturation of a kind that equipped them with sensibilities more fully developed than might otherwise be expected in this generation. Those who resumed their interrupted educational paths did so with a high level of independence of mind. These were not potential university students proceeding straight from secondary studies with little 'life experience', but mature young people who had served and survived a long world war, people with well-developed experience, ideas and expectations about culture and politics.

At the same time the path to a tertiary education was opened up to a socio-economic group who, before the war, could not have expected to have access to university. The Department of Post-War Reconstruction was set up in late 1942, and the Re-establishment and Employment

Act of 1945 set out entitlements, including employment preferences for ex-service personnel, and created the Commonwealth Reconstruction Training Scheme (CRTS) and the Commonwealth Employment Service. By the late 1940s, the system was at its peak, with more than 170,000 people receiving training under the scheme, of whom 20,000 were in university courses (Powell and MacIntyre 2015: 12–15).

> The Scheme provided training for ex-servicemen and women necessary for them to be reestablished in suitable civilian occupations. The last date for acceptance of applications was 30 June 1950 and by the middle of 1951 over 300,000 people had been accepted by the Scheme, making it one of the most significant strategies for social change in Australia. In order to be eligible for assistance under the Scheme, servicemen and servicewomen were required to have had a minimum of six months service and to have been honourably discharged . . . Training was available in one of three categories – professional, vocational or rural – and could be undertaken either full time or on a part time basis. Individuals embarking on full time training had tuition and other fees paid and received living allowances. (Commonwealth Reconstruction Training Scheme administrative records)

CRTS made a university education available to thousands of lower-income families (Powell and MacIntyre 2015: 83). Melbourne University and the Conservatorium became significant magnets for major figures in the post-war jazz scene, including Tony Newstead, Ken Ingram, Don Banks and George Tack (Sandford 2018: 61). According to trumpeter Tony Newstead, the concerts leading up to the first Australian

Jazz Convention in 1946 'had a university association' (Sandford 2018: 69). The sequence of military service then tertiary education during the 1940s was transformative for a generation of young people. Tasmanian pianist Ian Pearce recalled doing a course at the Melbourne Conservatorium under the army rehabilitation scheme: 'The army had changed my whole attitude to life' (Williams 1981: 30).

At the same time the population was increased and diversified by the arrival of free and assisted passage immigrants from the UK and an influx of European refugees. At the end of the Second World War there was a government-initiated mass migration programme. Between 1946 and 1960, this led to an annual increase in the population by 2.7 per cent per annum (Horne 2019: 42). This led to a broad sea change in the national ethnic profile that permeated and opened up attitudes and lifestyles, including artistic tastes, and even diet, especially among the younger generation.

The post-war developments in Australian culture, however, were sometimes ambiguous with regard to their social impact. One thread in the weave which surfaced in the decade or so following the conclusion of the war, and which was particularly manifested in the jazz culture, was a reversion to a pervasive masculinism. Since various sociopolitical developments going back to the late nineteenth century, and much accelerated during the interwar years with the rise of the 'New Woman', the balance in gender relations had gradually shifted through the twentieth century. While 'military modernity' during the First World War had scarred, maimed and killed a generation of young men, in the wake of the war, women had enjoyed massive emancipative benefits from 'civilian modernity', including a high degree of public participation in and formation of popular culture. In the 1920s, jazz in Australia was gendered as feminine, equated with the liberated young woman the flapper (see further Johnson 2023B: 9–11). Her social agency was fortified in many ways during the Second World War as women were called upon to fill spaces left vacant by the enlistment of menfolk.

With war's end, Australia entered a period of general conservatism, a desire to re-establish the comfortable ambience of earlier times. While one effect of this was to show in stronger relief the more progressive sociopolitical elements in society, this was also complemented by the attempt to re-balance gender relations in a resurgence of the masculinism that had been such a powerful strain in Australian settler society. The manifestations of this ranged from changes in 'couture, grooming, body shape and demeanour . . . away from the aggressive, quasi-androgynous image of the 1920s to an image of child-bearer and household nurturer . . . The man resumed his role as the breadwinner out in the public space; the member of the nuclear family who carried the final authority' (Johnson 2023C: 167).

While the emerging traditional jazz movement often overlapped with youthful political radicalism, as far as gender politics was concerned, it took on much of the complexion of a masculinism that could easily teeter over into misogyny. In spite of the major role women had played in what was understood to be jazz since its early years in Australia, including numerous all-female dance bands throughout the 1920s and during the war (Dreyfus 1999), the influential jazz advocate Bill Miller declared: 'there were few women in Melbourne who were able to talk intelligently about jazz . . . the number of women who could play a jazz instrument proficiently was negligible' (Sandford 2018: 66). In his memoir, echoing entrepreneur Horst Liepolt's maxim 'Der dames, dey don't dig der jazz', Dick Hughes declared, 'By and large the ladies don't get the spirit of jazz', and 'I have long since come to the reluctant conclusion that there is something in the feminine psyche that finds jazz repellent or, possibly, too competitive', and he continues to expatiate in this vein for another six pages (Hughes 1977: 84, 85, 85–91).

Much of the character and profile of the developing jazz community can be understood by reference to the broader musical context in Australia over this period. As one of the most influential figures in the post-war jazz movement, and a long-time colleague of John Sangster, Graeme Bell's experience is instructive in this respect. Bell was introduced to jazz by his brother Roger who, along with fellow students at Scots College, Bill 'Spadge' Davies and Ade Monsbourgh, had become interested in the music in the early 1930s. Hitherto, Bell's interests lay in 'classical' music; he found the popular music of the time 'trite and insipid', but was particularly interested in the idea of improvisation, which, like many of his generation, he felt was constrained by Swing, which was therefore somewhat disdained (Bell 1988: 28, 29, 32). He recalled that during the late 1930s members of the Musicians' Union and the Musicians' Club regarded their music as incomprehensible 'noise' made by imposters, in the context of the 'sweet block orchestrations of their dance orchestrations and the freedom of playing collective improvisation was something very foreign to them' (Bell 1988: 36). It is important to note, then, that this style of jazz was set in opposition, not to other jazz genres like 'modern' or 'bop', terms whose advent still lay in the future, but to current mainstream commercial dance orchestras.

Given this framing dynamic, it is not surprising that there was at that time negligible formal infrastructure in place through which to develop fluency in their chosen music. Sydney reed player Don Burrows recalled:

> When I and Errol Buddle, John Sangster and Bryce Rohde were on the way up, none of us had access to jazz studies programs, there were no such things. But what I, and they, did have was a different social environment as far as music was concerned. It afforded us as youngsters the opportunities to see as well as hear big bands. They were all over the place in those days, even the nightclub bands, with brass and four saxes . . . I'm a World War II development [*sic*] and we had to fly by the seat of our pants and I can't change my ways. I seem to respond at gut level. (Williams 1981: 60, 61)

Brisbane reed player Tich Bray, learning in the mid-1940s, remembered similarly:

> I didn't know anything about improvising so I had to do things the hard way. I had to get the chordal structure of the tune, get the record, play it over and over and over and copy the solos down note for note to find out what was going on. I did that with a lot of records, copying solos down to see what different musicians did on the chordal structure. (Sandford 2018: 21)

In the absence of any formal jazz education, learning how to play the music in Australia was thus a very ad hoc process, relying on a disparate and often discrete range of sources: radio, a 'trickle' of jazz records, some transcriptions in the US journal *Downbeat* (beginning in 1936), often reprinted in the local journal *Tempo*, some important individuals like Bill Miller, and live performances, such as at Melbourne's Fawkner Park Kiosk. Sound movies also provided a degree of exposure to contemporary US jazz-inflected popular music, as in *Hollywood Hotel* (1937), which included Benny Goodman's 'Sing, Sing, Sing', *The Birth of the Blues* (1941), with Jack Teagarden, and Movietone shorts, in which Brisbane drummer Sid Bromley saw the Washboard Rhythm Kings while serving in Port Moresby in 1942 (Sandford 2018: 19–21).

There was an upside to all this, from which I also benefited as a learner in the 1960s. Until the arrival of tertiary jazz education courses in the 1970s, and the more recent online access to virtually the entire archive of recorded jazz, the relative dearth of available music meant that what learners could actually get their hands on and share became note-for-note internalized from repeated playing. Perth-born Keith Hounslow, speaking of the glut of jazz material now available, recalled that in his days as a beginner, because there was so much less material available, 'we knew every nuance backwards and really savoured everything we came across' (Williams 1981: 66). This deep internalization of the traditional jazz corpus would become pervasive in Sangster's compositions and arrangements.

If we now narrow our focus to Melbourne, we shall discover nuances that localize the broad picture so far outlined.

Beginning with the obvious: Melbourne is not Sydney. The two state capitals have always been the major metropolitan centres for Australian jazz. But their respective histories have cast very different shadows over their twentieth-century profiles, particularly in relation to popular culture and music. That is certainly a case for extended studies, but they would touch on the origins of the two cities. Sydney was founded in 1788 as a penal settlement. Apart from administrators and a military contingent, the founding populace was literally made up of criminals, largely Anglo-Irish. Although subsequent convict ships also carried free settlers, the majority of these would become farmers outside the metropolis.

In the case of what would become Victoria, an early attempt to establish a convict settlement in 1802 was aborted. Melbourne was proclaimed a town in 1837 and a municipality in 1842. It was a free settlement, although in 1844 it also took in convicts ('exiles') deported from 'The Motherland' as cheap labour. When a convict ship entered Port Philip Bay just five years later, public outcry prohibited it from landing in Melbourne, and the ship proceeded to Sydney where its 295 convicts were absorbed into the community without ado (see further, Hughes 1987: 553–7). The 'convict stain' was to be a Sydney phenomenon.

With the discovery of gold in Victoria's Ballarat in 1851, as the nearest state capital city and export/import conduit, Melbourne became one of the world's wealthiest and most infrastructurally sophisticated cities, and the temporary commonwealth capital from Federation until the establishment of Canberra as the national capital in 1927. As Melbourne lost its economic dominance with the working out of the goldfields towards the end of the century and the 1890s Depression, Sydney pulled ahead of Melbourne economically from the early twentieth century (see further Johnson 2023A: 96–7). Sydney also experienced more frequent and direct contact with US culture, mainly through its position in relation to international shipping lanes, and this has been reflected in a closer orientation to US popular culture. In 1933–4 Sydney bandleader Jim Davidson's swing orchestra played a season in Melbourne, and the leader was struck by the resistance of more inhibited local dancers to his faster tempos and the dearth of jazz-inflected material in local repertoire (see further Johnson 2023A: 97–9).

In brief, if simplistic, summary, the ambience of Melbourne was, relative to Sydney, more conservative, genteel and less US-oriented. It was a culture in which radical and progressive movements would be more conspicuous (see further Horne 2019: 41), and with a stronger sensitivity to cultural 'transgressiveness' than in Sydney, where, for example, opportunities for employment for jazz musicians were much expanded by the gambling culture when it became the first state to legalize gaming machines in clubs in 1957. It was Melbourne that became the main metropolitan hub of the revivalist movement also for simple reasons of geography; it was central to the network linking Melbourne, Ballarat, Adelaide, Hobart and Launceston, within which frequent personal interactions took place.

It was out of this relatively staid culture that there was a surge of interest in jazz among the city's youth in Melbourne from the late 1930s into the war years (Bell 1988: 51–4), the city becoming 'a crucial centre of Australian jazz' (Johnson 1987:

205). A traditional jazz scene continued to flourish in post-war Melbourne, centred on such groups as the Bell brothers, then trumpeters Tony Newstead and Frank Johnson, and given a sense of community by general socializing, drinking together and home jam sessions in which there was cross-pollination between bands (Sandford 2018: 59–60). It was a tight-knit community, almost masonic in its exclusionary argot, and even nicknames. The point was made in a 2009 interview by pianist Timothy Stevens with publisher Bryony Cosgrove, on the subject of Sangster's memoir: 'Cosgrove: They've all got such fantastic nicknames . . . I don't know who most of these people are. Stevens: Well nobody outside of that circle would. Cosgrove: No, they wouldn't; it's a sort of a code, really' (Cosgrove interview 2009).

Drummer Len Barnard considered that the traditional scene in the late 1940s was,

> all Melbourne apart from the Port Jackson and Riverside band in Sydney. We always had a nice rapport in Melbourne. There might have been a bit of rivalry, but there was nothing with any spite in it, and we were all terribly good friends and used to socialise a lot. . . . Somebody would say 'There's a blow on', so we'd go and play with some of the other guys. (Williams 1981:16)

And: 'The whole Melbourne fraternity then was, um, quite lively. You know, there were lots of bands playing and er the Frank Johnson band was going pretty well and Graeme Bell' (Len Barnard interview 2003). The 'nice rapport' with 'the other guys' did not prevent internal cleavages. In the late 1940s, the mouldy vs modern factionalism was evident. On one occasion at a Southern Jazz Society gathering, clarinettist George Tack and pianist Will McIntyre spoke highly of Benny Goodman's jazz, and Tom Wanliss recalled, 'I thought that some of the young "Mouldy Fygges"[2] . . . would faint at these treasonable remarks' (Sandford 2018: 79). This cleavage was to a great extent a second-generation phenomenon, to which Sangster himself would fall victim in 1958 (see below, 'Sangster: The Life'). The first-generation musicians were more sparsely endowed with material, and therefore more eclectic and less able to indulge in such precious discriminations.

In general, Melbourne has maintained an extraordinarily high level of live music venues. A live music census in 2018 reported that the city enjoyed the world's highest number of such venues per capita, and according to the daily *Sydney Morning Herald*, 17 May 2019, Melbourne boasted 553 live music venues as compared with 453 in New York, 385 in Tokyo and 245 in London (Horne 2019: 11). And a significant proportion of this has been jazz. By 1950, Melbourne was enjoying a jazz boom, 'the pop music of the day' according to record producer Bill Armstrong, the 'New Orleans of the south', in trumpeter Frank Turville's words. The Saturday dances at The Powerhouse would attract nearly 1,000 dancers; the Cavalcade of Jazz concert at the Exhibition Building in May 1950 had an audience of 10,000 (Sandford 2018: 101).

The year 1950 arguably represented a peak in the Melbourne jazz scene, after which the music began to enter a slump, not helped by the 1949 coal strike, followed by a long public transport strike that affected social life. The jazz

---

[2] 'Mouldy Fygge' was a term used to describe the most purist of the traditionalists, who believed that the only 'true jazz' was recorded, mainly by Black musicians, in the 1920s.

'centre of gravity' gradually moved north to Sydney (Johnson 1987: 207) where by 1953 Graeme Bell noted there were three times as many jazz concerts and four times the commercial recording companies as Melbourne (Bell 1988: 113). It is perhaps no coincidence that this was the year both Bell and Sangster relocated northwards, likewise, for the first time, the annual Australian Jazz Convention which maintained the traditional jazz community on what became a national level (see below) was held not in Melbourne, but in Sydney.

Notwithstanding these changes, the perception of Melbourne as the centre of the traditional jazz movement has persisted to the present. Speaking in 1981, pianist Tony Gould declared: 'There is an enormous amount of traditional jazz in Melbourne but little contemporary outside of Brian Brown. I think Keith [Hounslow] and I are better known in Sydney. Melbourne is incredibly conservative, and Victoria is aptly named: and that is my explanation for why contemporary jazz hasn't made it here' (Williams 1981: 73). Similarly, in the same year, vibraphonist Alan Lee, like Gould a long-time collaborator with Sangster, said: 'At present, the Melbourne scene is pretty Dixieland and, in fact, has always been like that' (Williams 1981: 96). As recently as 2023, in the jazz journal *Dingo*, Adam Simmons wrote: 'Melbourne is a Mecca for jazz lovers . . . Jazz is embedded in Melbourne's musical DNA', and he describes Melbourne jazz as 'unique' (Simmons 2023: 53, 54). Drummer Niko Schäuble considers that the city has 'One of the most stable jazz scenes in Australia' (Simmons 2023: 53).[3]

---

[3] For a general historical overview of jazz in Melbourne, see Johnson 1987: 205–11.

From the outset, the Melbourne jazz community was, to a marked degree, largely sustained by 'amateur' musicians and enthusiasts (Bisset 1987: 121). As we shall see, this would have a number of consequences for the community ethos, including a DIY spirit and a consciousness of socio-cultural and political issues that went beyond music. Although the trade/professional profile of the musicians was very broad (see, for example, Johnson 2023A: 19), the jazz community was biased towards the middle and upper-middle class, and the University of Melbourne was a particularly rich source of musicians and patrons (Bell 1988: 43). Roger Bell recalled the 1930s as 'the days when Melbourne was a rather conservative society. . . . Most of the chaps who took up jazz were educated chaps with enquiring minds and I suppose it was a frustrating time for them and jazz music offered something exciting' (Sandford 2018: 15). Many of the participants in this revival were tertiary graduates; George Tack observed of Tony Newstead's band that 'with another degree or two the band could have formed half a thermometer' (Hughes 1977: 16). Pianist Dick Hughes was himself an undergraduate, majoring in Medieval French, and later graduated with BA (Hons) (Hughes 1977: 28, 34). Multi-instrumentalist Ade Monsbourgh, playing piano, along with other Melbourne jazz enthusiasts at the University of Melbourne, formed the 'Shop Swingers', then the University Rhythm Club (Bell 1988: 35). In 1962, at the 25th Anniversary Concert of the Melbourne University Rhythm it was noted in the *Melbourne Sun* that in Tony Newstead's band there were 'nine men who have between them 21 university degrees' (Sandford 2018: 125). In general, the jazz community manifested a high level of intellectual curiosity, an impulse towards autodidacticism that 'bodgied together' a uniquely eclectic body of knowledge.

When Sangster entered the scene in the 1940s, he was deeply both impressed and puzzled by this basically white middle-class movement, recalling in 1983:

> Here's all this American jazz, all these black musicians – it's a black music – and then the revival came in Melbourne, Australia. Why not Timbuktu? Why Melbourne, and for that matter why not Perth? I haven't figured it out. I don't know because when we were doing it we were white, Anglo-Saxon, Protestant, middle class, wearing white shirts to play our jazz music with the sleeves rolled down and buttoned up, not even rolled up. (Sandford 2018: 64)

The class profile was noted by singer (and pianist) Judy Durham, later of The Seekers, when she described her first visit to a jazz club: 'It was packed, not with slick-backed, greasy-haired, leather-jacketed rockers and their swinging skirt dancing girl-friends, but girls and boys in pressed shirts, duffle coats, cooks' daks and pointy toed shoes. They danced to music with a long history, music that asked to be respected' (Horne 2019: 77).

The burgeoning Melbourne traditional jazz scene was catalysed by particular individuals and a succession of 'marquee' events, with most of which Sangster would become closely associated. Graeme Bell was so central to the jazz community that as recently as 2023, more than a decade after his death at the age of ninety-seven, Adam Simmons speculated on his influence on the continuing vitality of traditional jazz in Melbourne (Simmons 2023: 54). Sangster's musical collaboration with Bell would be, at about a decade and a half, the longest of his career.

The lives and careers of Graeme Bell and members of his coterie, notably his brother Roger and Ade Monsbourgh, are recorded in detail in Graeme's own memoir of 1988. He and his colleagues were not only central to the emerging jazz movement but closely involved with a broader radical network that embraced major representatives of modernism in the arts, such as Sidney Nolan, the 'Heide' group, the Contemporary Art Society, writer Max Harris, and political organizations, including the Eureka Youth League. The members of this informal community regularly gathered in particular Melbourne pubs and restaurants, especially Italian and Chinese, and established something of an artistic 'colony' at Eltham, about twenty kilometres northeast of Melbourne's CBD (see, for example, Bell 1988: 36–7, 43–5; see further Johnson 2023A). In a very conservative Melbourne, all these quasi-bohemian 'fringe dwellers' and their lifestyles stood out in strong relief.

We have noted that Graeme Bell's interest in jazz was sparked by his brother Roger. They opened an account with American Milt Gabler of Commodore Records in New York, which made available to them contemporary jazz musicians in the traditional style. Gradually they became involved with a local network of like-minded collectors (Bell 1988: 32). The two formed a small band for dances, though initially, they played little jazz. The main venue for hearing live jazz performances was the Fawkner Park Kiosk on Sunday afternoons, where 'veterans', including Benny Featherstone, Bob Tough, Frank Coughlan, Mickey Walker, George Silker, Bert Cooper, Alf Warne, Neville Maddison and Larry Keane, played 'gutsy jazz' (Bell 1988: 33).

In due course, their jazz orientation was increased by the addition of other jazz-interested musicians. One night coming home from a dance gig, they overheard a clarinet playing a blues, coming from Saul's Coffee Lounge in Kew. They went in and introduced themselves to Don 'Pixie' Roberts, who joined them for what would be the next fifteen years. With the addition of drummer Russ Murphy, whom they heard at a musical 'get together' at his home in Balwyn, they now formed the Portsea Four at Christmas time, 1940, playing at the Nepean Hotel Portsea (Bell 1988: 34–5). The band later expanded further with shifting personnel and numbers, including multi-instrumentalist Ade Monsbourgh, whose work on valve trombone later led US trumpeter Kaminsky to call him the Brad Gowans of Australia (Hughes 1977: 7). In 1945, they were joined by bassist Lou Silbereisen (Bell 1988: 57), who would later introduce Sangster to the Bell band after hearing him at the Alan Watson 'party' (see below).

One characteristic that seems distinctive to Melbourne is the extent of the DIY jazz culture of the revivalist movement. 'After all, if you've got something to market and a ready-made outlet does not present itself, you create your own' (Bell 1988: 41). The band hired a function room, Leonard's Cabaret, in St Kilda for Sunday nights, printed their own tickets, and made their patrons members of a club in order to circumvent restrictive licencing laws. With the growing popularity of the events, they formed the Victorian Jazz Lovers' Society, drew up a mailing list and held functions at the Stage Door in Flinders Street where they kicked off on 9 August 1941 with a programme called 'History of Jazz'. 'To date, this was probably the most adventurous staging of jazz music in Melbourne. It was co-produced by Harry Stein of the Eureka Youth League under the banner of the Victorian Jazz Lovers, although they had to suspend activities in January 1942 because the wartime Universal Training Scheme (the 'call-up') destabilized the community (Bell 1988: 41, 43).[4]

Gradually, the major ballrooms featured small jazz bands in alternation with the house orchestras. While there were other bands and orchestras that included some jazz material, what distinguished the Bell coterie was its exclusive commitment to 'collective improvisation in the classic jazz mould' (Bell 1988: 42). Having been playing dances for the Eureka Hot Jazz Society at Queensberry Street North Melbourne, the band established a regular Saturday night cabaret and called it the Uptown Club, opening on 29 June 1946. This was again very DIY, with wives and friends attending to front of house and décor, the latter including rising artists and stage designers Tony Underhill and Warwick Armstrong (Bell 1988: 56). The band made their first recordings – six sides – with a major label, Regal Zonophone, in 1947 in Sydney. They sold over 50,000 copies each, 'by today's standards, gold – or even platinum' (Bell 1988: 62). By the time of the band's departure for its first extended European tour on 3 July 1947, it had established itself as the pre-eminent representative of the jazz movement. Sangster began his public performance career at the Uptown Club and would be a member of the Bell band for its second European tour.

---

[4]The same DIY spirit is recorded in relation to the later Frank Johnson Fabulous Dixielanders' highly successful events organized at the Maison de Luxe (Sangster 1988: 36).

The Melbourne jazz culture would also be significantly enriched by another fortuitously placed individual, Bill Miller. Miller had studied law at Oxford before the war and on his return to Australia he had brought with him a collection of hundreds of classic jazz recordings that he had accumulated while in England (Johnson 1987: 212–13). The collection gave members of the Melbourne jazz fraternity direct access to a jazz archive unique in Australia. One member of that fraternity, Ray Marginson, recalled:

> He had this wall full of great records, and I was one of quite a few who got my jazz education at Bill's house . . . his great collection was a real honeypot for all jazz people. Nobody else had a collection like that in Melbourne. The great ambition of all young fans was to get to Bill's place to a record session. (Sandford 2018: 64)

The radius of the influence of this collection and Miller's deep knowledge of the field was increased as far as Tasmania when Miller was invited by 3UZ to script a thirty-minute jazz programme, which was to run weekly under the name *Jazz Night*, and later *Swing Night,* for two-and-a-half years (Sandford 2018: 23–4).

He also established Ampersand Records, specializing in recording Australian jazz. Dick Hughes describes the appearance of its first release in 1943, the two sides, 'Ja Da' and 'Oh That Sign' by Roger Bell's Jazz Gang and Don Roberts' Wolf Gang, with Max Kaminsky, as markers that 'Australian revivalist jazz had come of age' (Hughes 1977: 8).[5] Miller also established

---

[5] Hughes gives the release date as 1946, but Mitchell gives the recording date as 19 September 1943 (Mitchell 1988: 47)

an indispensable forum for jazz discussion when he founded the journal called *Jazz Notes* in 1941. Unlike Sydney's *Tempo* and *Music Maker*, which were for the broader dance band profession, *Jazz Notes* was a specialist jazz magazine, which 'often gave us readers the first biographical and discographical details of musicians who had hitherto been known only by name and sometimes by their music'. In 1946, Miller launched a second influential journal, the *Australian Jazz Quarterly*. Graeme Bell named him as the most important figure in the band's early successes (Bell 1988: 31, 62).

A strange episode that also provided a centre for the formation of the Melbourne jazz community was the extended Alan Watson 'jazz party'. Watson had inherited a mansion in South Yarra from his parents; stocked with wine cellars and musical instruments, the house became both a permanent drop-in centre or party and, in the case of Sangster, an informal residence for jazz musicians (Linehan interview 1979). By Sangster's recollections, it lasted for eighteen months (Johnson interview 1988), or two (Sangster 1988: 29) or three years (Beilby interview 1999; see also Stevens 2009: 12). It was evidently well underway by August 1949, as Sangster recalls US cornetist and Ellington alumnus Rex Stewart being present (Sangster 1988: 17); Stewart arrived in Australia to work with Graeme Bell on 8 August of that year (Bell 1988: 129). Sangster waxes lyrical and at length about this in his often unreliable memoir (Sangster 1988: 16–33), but the ambience is confirmed in the following extended extract from an interview conducted by Timothy Stevens (TM) with trumpeter Keith Hounslow (KH), beginning with a reference to Sangster and Shirley Drew, who would marry in 1949:

**KH:** They were just there, and they used to live in the garage, as I write in my thing [*My Jazz Life*], out the back, which was a three-car or four-car garageand it had this beaut big billiard room built on the top, and Watson let them stay out there even when the party situation was diminishing, John lived on there[6] . . .

. . .

**TS:**   So as the party wound down.

**KH:**  Yes well you could say that. But then what would happen, you'd be stuck one night, and we'd say, 'well look, what'll we do?' and we'd meet with Warwick Dyer and people like that too, and we'd say 'what'll we do? Well let's go to Watson's.' You didn't ring up, you'd just turn up, and invariably there'd be two or three there or someone or another there, and you'd get something going again, you see? Play all the bloody time, we used to play all night and things, you know, blues, and God knows what, the same limited music, but we thought it was great, and had a lot of fun.

. . .

**KH:**  It wound down, . . . that's how it happened. And you could keep going back there for years, and find it, as I remember it . . .

. . .

**KH:**  Food used to be going on at all [hours] . . . And the cellar was stocked with the most exotic champagnes and things that were years old then, you know, and it was a very wonderful thing, and you went down to this long cellar under the house, and Sangster, as he said, we drank our way through the cellar, and ate our way through the larder; and this larder, was all exotic things from overseas, and all

---

[6]Confirmed in Sangster 1988: 31.

things, in cans, and we'd be there at night, and someone would say, 'you feel hungry?' You know, we used to go on like this, 'you feel hungry old chap? Well I'll just go down and get something to eat.' And come back with an armful of stuff. And there'd be people eating at three o'clock in the morning, you know, and all this sort of thing.

. . .

**TS:** Somebody should write a book about *that*. That party, you know. If they could get everybody who's still around who was there, just to talk about it. I mean, what an education. What a sort of ferment, all those young enthusiastic musicians living together, with the food and the wine taken care of, and no noise restrictions. (Hounslow interview 2007)

The most influential and durable event in the formation of a national jazz community, however, was another Melbourne initiative, the annual Australian Jazz Convention (AJC), inaugurated in the week between Boxing Day and New Year's Eve, 1946, and still going, in that week, more than six decades on. It is the world's oldest surviving annual jazz festival. We have been drawing up a broad profile of the Melbourne jazz community during the 1940s; it was this generation who led the way in the foundation of the AJC, born out of a convergence of many of the forces we have reviewed. These include the DIY spirit of the immediate post-war, often ex-service, generation of enthusiasts, the wartime discovery that there was, in fact, a burgeoning national jazz community, the energy of particular individuals, a number of whom had leftist inclinations, and the momentum created by various key episodes outlined above. The origins and history have been set out in detail and need not be repeated here (see Johnson 1987: 87–90, and in greater detail Johnson 2023A: 2–26). It was attended by delegates from as far afield as Adelaide, Hobart and Sydney, and consisted of concerts, jam sessions and 'band battles', a riverboat excursion, a street parade and formal talks on jazz, all covered extensively by the press. Suffice in this context to say that the event was inspirational in the continuing consolidation of the Australian, traditionally oriented jazz movement. Graeme Bell had been prominent in the discussions leading to its initiation, along with Ade Monsbourgh and editor of *Jazz Notes* C. Ian Turner; Adelaide pianist, trombonist and composer Dave Dallwitz; and amateur drummer and representative of the leftist Eureka Youth League Harry Stein. Bell wrote of that first AJC:

> It is impossible to describe the euphoria of that first jazz convention. Here were these musicians from Hobart and Adelaide [no established bands from Sydney were represented in full] – few of us had previously met – who had been searching out this music as we had. Their aims were the same and they talked the same language. The rapport was almost unbelievable. Friendships were made in that Christmas of 1946 that have remained firm as a rock ever since. (Bell 1988: 61)

The following year, Perth-born trumpeter Keith Hounslow attended the second, and recalled: 'I walked three feet off the ground . . . I couldn't believe that there were all these people playing jazz' (Hounslow interview 2007).

And it was in the forum of the Australian Jazz Convention that the rising star John Sangster first came to national attention.

# **2**  Sangster
## The life

Born John Grant Sangster[1] on 17 November 1928 at Moira Private Hospital, Sandringham, Victoria, his parents were Isabella Dunn Sangster (*née* Davidson) from Perth, Scotland, born on 26 May 1890, and John Sangster from Aberdeen, Scotland, born on 10 September 1896. They arrived in Australia on the same ship on 18 May 1922. They married on 6 September 1927, following the death of Isabella's first husband, James Pringle, on 18 August 1927, an interval of only three weeks, prompting speculation that they were already known to each other. The family lived in Sandringham, a bayside suburb some 16 kilometres south of the Melbourne CBD, where the young John attended Sandringham Primary School from 3 October 1933, moving to the local primary school when the family moved to Glenburnie Road, Vermont, 20 kilometres east of the CBD in 1935 or 1936, and then onto Box Hill Secondary School, also to the east of the CBD (Bisset interview 1977). In 1946 he began a civil engineering diploma course at Melbourne

---

[1] The main outlines for the following account are from an unpublished timeline compiled by Timothy Stevens, which he kindly made available to me, and his 28 November 2013 online article 'The Death of Isabella Dunn Sangster', available at http://timstevens.com.au/the-death-of-isabella-dunn-sangster/ Accessed 5 June 2015. This and all other sources are identified in the Reading List.

Technical School, but dropped out before the completion of his first year.

During his teen years, he showed an active interest in music, perhaps as early as 1943, drumming on various surfaces (Stevens 2009: 5, 6) such as the tyres of his upturned bicycle, using drumsticks he stole from the Vermont Scout Troop which he attended (Sangster 1988: 1). He started on the trombone, then the cornet bought with money stolen from his father's wallet,[2] (Sangster 1988: 2) and listened to jazz recordings on a gramophone kept in the laundry outhouse. These included the Graeme Bell Zonophones (Bisset interview 1977). As these were recorded in 1947, Sangster would have been nineteen, and he had formed a band that included his friend Sid Bridle, practising at Bridle's home in the adjacent suburb of Forest Hill.

Although the young Sangster appears to have been reserved and withdrawn (Stevens 2009: 2), on occasions he displayed evidence of inner disturbance. On 10 January 1946, he pleaded guilty in the Box Hill court to three charges of arson, admitting to 'having splashed kerosene over a tea-tree hedge and a fence post and then setting fire to them. He had also set fire to a telephone directory. He did not know why he had done so and bore no one any grudge'. The report in the Melbourne *Herald* reported that leniency was urged as the

--------

[2] As in most instruments, Sangster was largely self-taught, although, as noted, as a condition of his joining the Bell band, he was required to take lessons. He also took some instruction on drums from Charlie Blott (Sangster 1988: 20), as well as from an Indian master drummer, and also one lesson on cornet (Bisset 1987: 166; Sangster 1988: 18, 129–30). He once sought lessons on the vibes from Bruce Findlay, but who found that 'I can't bear to watch you play, you're doing it all wrong' (Sangster 1988: 229).

accused was 'at a critical age . . . [he] had been getting up at 5am to sell papers before attending school' (Stevens 2013).

Sangster began attending the jazz functions held at the Uptown Club, which opened in June 1946. Although his mother, Isabella, was evidently a capable pianist, playing Chopin on the family piano, she was hostile to her son's jazz activities. On 21 September 1946, at the family home, John (aged seventeen) killed Isabella (aged fifty-six) with an axe. Court records and recollections of family and friends speak of a dominating and ill-tempered woman with a very withdrawn husband (see further Stevens 2009: 2). At the trial, evidence was presented of her chronic bullying of her son. According to police and court records and prolific press reports, tensions came to a head on this day when, in spite of having been apparently given permission to go to the Uptown Club, his mother then refused to allow him and locked him out of the house. He broke back in with an axe, and in the ensuing confrontation, which according to one account included her attacking her son with a broom, bludgeoned her to death. At the trial on 9 and 10 December, he was acquitted of both murder and manslaughter, largely on grounds of provocation. Unsurprisingly, given the good-time persona he sought to present in his memoir, there is no reference to this and, in fact, the only mention of Isabella is to 'mither' and that she came from Perth, Scotland (Sangster 1988: 56).[3]

---

[3] Sangster's psychological relationships with women appear to have been, to say the least, ambivalently balanced between the swaggering masculinism of his times and something like dependency. In spite of reports of violence in his relationship with 'Bo', his *Requiem* album dedicated to her is movingly tender (see below), and this, in combination with his apparently off-hand comment

Shortly after his acquittal he attended the first Australian Jazz Convention (AJC) from 26 to 30 December 1946.[4] Here, the bands he heard included those of Graeme Bell and Tony Newstead and the South Australian band the Southern Jazz Group (Linehan 1981: [4]). He recalls his first gig as a cornet player being a university ball in a band led by George Tack and claims to have played at the first AJC in 1946 at age eighteen (Sangster 1988: 9). He attended the second AJC where he participated in some of the informal jam sessions (Stevens 2009: 7). There is a photograph of him on a truck watching a band playing at the second AJC in 1947 ( Johnson 1987: 89).

It was at the third AJC, 1948, held at the New Theatre in Flinders Street that he came to prominence as a young hot cornettist, playing with Sydney's Riverside Jazz Band, whose regular cornet player was unable to make the journey south. He made a strong impression, and Graeme Bell presented him with a cheque for five pounds as the most promising player (Bebbington 1997: 502; Linehan 1981: [4]). He recorded on cornet with Warwick Dyer's Stompers on 30 December, then with John Sangster's Jazz Six the next day, the dates and multi-state line-ups suggesting that these groups were formed out of AJC attendees (Mitchell 1988: 4, 83, 185; see further Stevens 2009: 4). By 1949, his Jazz Six had stabilized with an all-Melbourne line-up and performed at a Melba Memorial fund-raiser in May (Johnson 1987: 250). They then recorded

---

that she 'up and died on me', but that I 'lost interest in quite a lot of things for a while' (Sangster 1988: 202) is a slightly dissonant tonal convergence. He speaks of the appeal of the 'motherly touch' of buxom barmaids and owned a Kombi van which he called 'The Orange Womb' (Sangster 1988: 194, 242).

[4] All the foregoing, except as otherwise indicated, draws on Stevens 2013.

with an additional musician as John Sangster's Jazz Seven in September 1949 (Mitchell 1988: 185; and Stevens 2009: 9, which documents Sangster's early recording activities more generally).

At around this time, the legendary Alan Watson 'party' began. It was there that Sangster met Shirley Drew, aka by Sangster as 'Stinky' (Sangster 1988: 28), and the couple married on 18 November 1949 at the Church of Christ, Malvern, Caulfield, Victoria.[5] On the marriage certificate, his age is given as twenty-one, hers as twenty; his address is 23 Rockley Road South Yarra, which is the address of the Alan Watson party, and hers is 23 Seyb[illegible]eiley Road Caulfield; his occupation is listed as 'musician' and hers as the unfortunate term 'calculating operator'.

At this time Sangster was playing cornet and 'a tiny bit of drums' on a primitive kit (Beilby interview 1999; Linehan interview 1979; on his early work as a drummer, see Stevens 2009). He became active on the local revivalist scene and performed and recorded at the 1949 AJC, on 30 December (Mitchell 1988: 4). Graeme Bell's bass player Lou Silbereisen (who had been one of the witnesses listed in the marriage certificate referred to above) had heard Sangster playing rather rudimentary drums at Alan Watson's and, recognizing his potential, recommended him to Graeme Bell, who took him into the band on the condition that he take formal lessons from two erstwhile Bell drummers, Jack Banston and Russ Murphy (Bell 1988: 139). Sangster developed quickly

---

[5]Timothy Stevens, 2015, reports that he was unable to find evidence confirming Sangster's own account of the wedding.

enough to join the band as its drummer for a four-month multi-state Australian tour in the second half of 1950 (Bell 1988: 141–1). Together with the fact that he recorded on drums with Roger Bell's Pagan Pipers on 24 July 1950 (Mitchell 1988: 47), in assessing the veracity of Sangster's accounts of his life, it is notable that this conflicts with his own claim that he taught himself drums during the voyage on the *Orion* (see, for example, Sangster 1988: 48; Bisset 1987: 164) that departed on 25 October 1950. It carried with it the Graeme Bell band, plus a number of band wives, including Shirley (Bell 1988: 142), 'My wonderful long legged, long-haired blond comes-from-nordic-stock brand-spanking-new wife' (Sangster 1988: 49), to their second UK/European tour, which would last for sixteen months.

Highlights of the tour included two Royal Command performances with the Bell band, BBC broadcasts and a number of recording sessions with Sangster playing both drums/percussion and cornet, and recordings made in 1951 in Dusseldorf with Big Bill Broonzy (Mitchell 1988: 38, 39, 40, 53). Like Bell and his coterie, Sangster strongly believed that Australian jazz musicians should compose for their own repertoire, and it was during that tour that he began seriously composing, including for recordings with Bell and English trumpeter Humphrey Lyttelton (Bisset interview 1987; Linehan interview 1979; Mitchell 1988: 40). His time in the UK also introduced him to Kenny Graham's Afro-Cubists, and the Johnny Dankworth band, which turned his attention to more progressive jazz styles (Bisset interview 1987).

A regular association with Graeme Bell would continue for the next decade, and details are provided in Bell (1988), based in turn on the latter's meticulously maintained diaries and press clippings, held in Sydney's Mitchell library. The band returned to Australia, arriving in Melbourne on 15 April 1952, and four days later began a tour for the ABC, starting in the Sydney Town Hall on 19 April (Bell 1988: 181, 184). Sangster remained with the band for concerts, recordings and broadcasts, but the hectic commitments began to tell, particularly in relation to the members' families and former professional lives. In Yass, in the midst of a tour that had been plagued by vehicle breakdowns and heavy floods, on 6 June, the band agreed to break up, except for gigs in Melbourne, at the end of July 1952, while Bell and Sangster continued as professionals (Bell 1988: 187).

With Sangster alternating between trumpet and drums, there was nightclub work, recording and Australian and international tours, including, in 1954–5, Japan and Korea (see further detail, Bell 1988: 198–214). On returning to Australia in March 1955, the pair based themselves in Brisbane, with intervals in Sydney, Melbourne, South Australia and other parts of Queensland. In Brisbane Sangster took up the vibraphone while they played nightclub residencies at the Celebrity Club and the Blue Moon cabaret (Bell 1988: 215, 240; Len Barnard interview 2003). Over the next three years, both musicians would experience a succession of personal crises that, given their peripatetic musical careers over the previous five years, is hardly surprising. Sangster, in particular, seemed to be undergoing something of a breakdown. Bell wrote of this period as 'a hairy time for us all. Southerners seem to go mad when they get to Brisbane, or they did in those days. They were really wild days which I wouldn't like to repeat. We all drank too much. And Sangster got out of a car doing thirty-five miles an hour one night and nearly killed himself' (Williams 1981: 5–6.)

Graeme Bell's personal life was stabilized when he formed a relationship with Dorothy Gough (Bell 1988: 238), although she was careful to maintain a platonic distance until his divorce from his current wife Liz was finalized. After prolonged discussions, Liz and Graeme agreed on a separation in around 1957, then to a divorce, and Dorothy and Graeme would marry on 2 December 1961 (Bell 1988: 245, 264).

In the meantime, while Graeme was finding his feet, over 1956/7, Sangster's personal life was becoming increasingly chaotic. Sangster formed an association with a woman from Sydney known as Peggy (presumably Kathleen Margaret Therese Anne Kaiser, whom Shirley would name in her papers filing for divorce (Divorce papers, John and Shirley Sangster[6])). Peggy phoned him frequently from Sydney, via the number of the landlady of his serviced room in Upper Edward Street, Spring Hill (where Graeme was also lodging). This happened three times in one night up to 4.00 am from what was obviously a roaring party. Sangster was evicted (Bell 1988: 237). He was drinking heavily and becoming increasingly disorganized, arriving at gigs dishevelled, on one occasion in bare feet, hocking his trumpet to pay his fares to Melbourne to discuss divorce with Shirley, and having his drum kit repossessed (Bell 1988: 238, 239, 244). According to Bell, Sangster was 'in a very bad way mentally and physically' so he hitch-hiked to Melbourne in late 1956, staying with sculptor Clem Meadmore

_______________

[6]The citation 'Divorce Papers' refers to a collection incorporating a compilation of documents as detailed in the Reading List.

in Toorak, eventually joined by Peggy, both of them settling into day jobs (Bell 1988: 244).

During Dorothy Gough's first visit to Sydney, she was overwhelmed by the metropolitan glamour and evidently also moved in social circles that included Sangster's wife. She wrote from 229 Darlinghurst Road Kings Cross to Graeme in Queensland, making reference to Shirley Sangster, overheard discussing 'husband trouble'. In another letter to Graeme, undated but probably around August 1956, she wrote:

> Your news about Johnny is very disturbing. I can see no solution to all his problems until he himself can be brought to a realisation that to live in this civilised world responsibilities must be faced, and accepted, and that only after they have been dealt with are people really free in their minds to live [erasure] a full and *enjoyable* (I stress the word 'enjoyable') life.
>
> I feel that in spite of his bravado & seeming indifference, Johnny is probably worried about his inability to conform, but is powerless to do anything about it. You can't help him, nor can I or anyone else. It is something he will have to work out for himself and I only hope for his sake he can do it, or he will be a misfit all his life.
>
> I won't mention any of this to Shirley, as I don't want to interfere in any way.[7]

---

[7] All the Bell-related correspondence cited here is held in the Mitchell Library, Sydney NSW, Bell Box 4, BELL ML 1771/93, 4 (34). It is noteworthy that of all the many women he refers to in his memoir, the only one named and given the salutation accorded to so many of his male friends is Dorothy, who got Graeme 'back on the rails': 'On yer Dorothy' (Sangster 1988: 96).

Shirley petitioned for divorce on 15 April 1957 at the Divorce Registry NSW, giving her address as 40 Mona Road, Darling Point. Grounds adverted to are adultery with Kathleen Margaret Therese Anne Kaiser. Sangster's current address is given as Flat 8 Springfield Inn, Darlinghurst Road, Kings Cross (Divorce papers, John and Shirley Sangster). Shirley asserted that Sangster had deserted her when he left for Brisbane. She deposed that,

> early in 1955 in the course of his profession he went on tour to Japan entertaining troops.[8] On his return I noticed that he was indifferent towards me and unless he could obtain a position in his profession he refused to work at other occupations [Here there is the handwritten annotation 'other than for short periods', initialled by the JP] I had purchased a house for us and was working in two positions to endeavour to repay the purchase moneys.[9]

> During the first week in January 1956 the respondent told me he was leaving to take a position in Brisbane for a short period. He did not return and I went to Brisbane and saw him. During the course of conversation he said to me 'When I left you in January I intended to desert you and I do not intend to live with you again. I intend to follow my profession throughout Australia'. (Divorce papers, John and Shirley Sangster)

---

[8] This conflicts with Bell's account mentioned above, which I am inclined to think is more reliable.
[9] The document says that Sangster deserted her from 4 Cromwell Place, South Melbourne.

The required term of desertion was a minimum of three years, hence the interval between the original petition and the decree absolute. The divorce nisi was dated 3 June 1959 in the NSW Supreme Court, on grounds of at least three years desertion, beginning January 1956 when he left for Brisbane. It was undefended, and the decree absolute was granted on 17 September 1959 (Divorce papers, John and Shirley Sangster).

In the meantime, 'Peggy', named in the divorce papers, seems to disappear from the record, and later at some point, back in Sydney, Sangster established a relationship and cohabited with Janice Patricia Byrnes, whom he always referred to as 'Bo Diddley', after the US blues artist. As in other cases, in 1963 he 'steals' her from another man, a 'drummer mate', whom she is about to accompany to Melbourne to marry. Sangster and she steal away from a dinner, they 'got sprung', and the offended drummer refused to return the Bix records Sangster had lent him. The couple got married in Melbourne, but she returns to Sydney 'unmarried. Sort of' and the two moved together into a Kings Cross flat (Sangster 1988: 107–8). Little is known of Byrnes' background other than that her father was George Byrnes, her mother Jesse, née Wakeham, and she had been formerly married to Michael Hughes at the age of twenty-one (Byrnes 1980). She evidently shared his accommodation above El Rocco (see below) and was present when I played the private party with Sangster in around 1972, referred to in my Introduction. There are unattributable references to episodes of violence in the relationship, though Sangster would later dedicate a moving album to her, *Requiem (for a Loved One)* in 1980 (Mitchell 1988: 189).

Sangster joined Bell in December 1956 for a South Australian tour, then a little later for an engagement in Caloundra, Queensland (Bell 244, 245). They were still in Caloundra on 29 January 1957 (Bell Papers; Bell 1988: 245). The two of them went to Sydney for a residency at the Bennelong Hotel in Beverly Hills, arriving on Sunday 3 February 1957 (Bell 1988: 246), and starting at the Bennelong on 25 February, after two weeks at the Allawah Hotel until the Bennelong's current band contract ran out (Bell 1988: 246).[10] They were on a succession of six-month contracts, ending in around February 1959. Those two years were a relatively stable period both professionally and, apparently, personally.

At the Bennelong they played little jazz, mostly current hits and talent quests. Given their prominence as jazz musicians, it is notable that, throughout their careers, both Bell and Sangster often performed and recorded non-jazz repertoire as professional pub and cabaret musicians. Later, Bell says that it was not until 'halfway through the second year' (i.e. around mid-1958) that, with an augmented band for two nights a week (Sangster moving to trumpet and vibes), they began to 'sneak' jazz in whenever they could (Bell 1988: 254). After the two-year engagement at the Bennelong, however, Bell had become 'resigned to the fact that I would never again play jazz for a living' (Bell 1988: 255).

In the meantime, they maintained a busy musical schedule, including in April their first TV show on ABC. With Bell's band,



___________

[10] Bell received a letter dated 14 February at 209 Victoria Kings Cross – see Bell Box 4, BELL ML 1771/93, 4 (34), so he is certainly established there by then – he has 'a small but cosy room' (Bell 1988: 249).

Sangster was the drummer on recordings of several current hit songs, including 'The Pub with No Beer' and 'Kisses Sweeter than Wine' with Johnny Ashcroft in early 1958, then in May and October 1958 (Mitchell 1988: 5, 6). Skiffle was enjoying a wave of popularity, led by the UK jazz trombonist/bandleader Chris Barber's alumnus, guitarist/vocalist Lonnie Donegan. Bell recorded a number of skiffle hits, including 'Rock Island Line' (with Sangster on washboard), which made the top ten and paved the way for increasing radio and TV dates, and playing support for the Johnny Ray tour (Bell 1988: 251). At the end of the year, the skiffle group was voted top act of the year along with Horrie Dargie by the *Daily Mirror*, and the Sydney *Sun* newspaper voted 'Freight Train' the best Australian record of the year.

He returned to the 'mouldy fygge' traditional jazz scene at the end of 1958, when he recorded on drums with the Bell-Monsbourgh Group in Sydney on December 29 (Mitchell 1988: 42). Clearly, however, since his first spectacular appearance at the AJC a decade earlier, Sangster's stylistic palette had broadened, and this became particularly evident at the 1958 AJC. Having performed Ellington's 'It Don't Mean a Thing', the musicians were 'politely informed that they weren't entirely welcome as they were too modern. "I got banned – I was barred. Up till then I thought I was a traddie, just a jazz musician"' ([Linehan 1981: 4]).[11] That Sangster was becoming

---

[11] In his memoir, Sangster recalls playing with the Bell Band at the seventh AJC [1952], performing big-band numbers like 'The Mooche', 'King Porter Stomp', 'Jersey Lightning', and the band being reprimanded by the organizers for playing 'big-band' music and using saxes (Sangster 1988: 82).

far more than just a 'traddie' would become increasingly apparent.

Sangster continued with Bell until at least 1 September 1959 when the band (with Sangster on trumpet) played a royal ball for Princess Alexandra in Rockhampton, Queensland (Bell 1988: 257). Following a 'short season' at Mick Moylan's pub in Dolls Point (Bell 1988: 255), however, after what Bell recalled was nine-and-a-half years, the two musicians embarked on separate paths that would, nonetheless, frequently intersect. Sangster wrote arrangements for Bell's Sylvania Hotel (Sydney) season that began in late 1959, although he was not in the band (Bell 1988: 258, 259); he also performed on vibes as a guest on Bell's later TV show *Trad Dad* (Bell 1988: 271) and appeared on the final show after a twelve-month run on 24 June 1963 (Bell 1988: 281). Bell himself, however, had invested in an art gallery[12] and had ceased looking for music work, so Sangster went out freelancing on his own. He made a number of recordings with Sydney's venerable Port Jackson Jazz Band (Mitchell 1988: 169; Mitchell 2002: 94), and also joined the Ray Price Quartet on cornet, remaining into the early 1960s. But, through the 1960s, he enlarged his attention to composing and arranging for studio session work, including for TV, notably the Eric Jupp programme, *The Magic of Music* (Linehan interview 1979; mistakenly referred to as *The Sound of Music* in Bisset 1987: 165), which enjoyed international popularity

---

[12]Bell maintained a lifelong interest in art; he had received lessons from prominent painter Max Meldrum in the late 1930s (Bell 1988: 36–7), and continued to produce work throughout his lifetime; I have one of his works from 1994 on my wall.

during its run from 1961 to 1974. He composed jingles for advertising and film and television music.

Although, as a performer, he remained audible in the traditional jazz community, as for example with Ray Price, he was also becoming significant in more progressive movements. The range was illustrated through recording activity from 1963 to 1966, as trumpeter, percussionist and vibraphonist, that included releases with Ray Price, 1930s veteran bandleader/trombonist/trumpeter Frank Coughlan, progressive and modernist musicians such as Lyn Christie, Judy Bailey and Don Burrows, as well as his own groups (Mitchell 1988: 10, 43, 57, 71, 171; Mitchell 1998: 43, 212; Mitchell 2002: 28, 103). Most notably, he immersed himself in the modern to experimental community through his involvement with Australia's most important incubator of 'modern' jazz, which had opened in 1955, the El Rocco nightclub in Kings Cross.[13] He was playing the venue by 1962 (Bisset interview 1977[14]), becoming a fixture among the performers in a number of bands, including his own. In his memoir, he cited the Alan Watson party and the 'El Rocco decade and a half' as the most significant 'to the development and nurturing of our "Modern" jazz music, and especially of our modern jazz musos. So much that I love came out of these two Nurseries' (Sangster 1988: 141). His association with the venue would be strengthened

---

[13] On El Rocco, see further Johnson January/February 1983, March/April 1983, May/June 1983; Clare 1995. In his memoir, Sangster recalls moving into a 'Penthouse' in William Street, Kings Cross with Bo in 1965 (Sangster 1988: 131).
[14] Although in his memoir he dates the beginning of his performances at El Rocco to June 1960, with Col Nolan (ldr./piano) and bassist Gerry Gardiner (Sangster 1988: 134).

when he rented accommodation at the top of the building that housed El Rocco in its basement (Bebbington 1997: 502).

In 1966, he was inspired by Bob James, Sarah Vaughan's accompanist on her Australian tour (Johnson interview 1988). James introduced Sangster to the work of Albert Ayler, Sun Ra, Cecil Taylor, and the deployment of extraneous noises, *sons trouvés*. This led him towards experimental work involving total improvisation for the ABC. With Sangster on drums, Bob Gebert (piano) and Ron Carson (bass), the musicians responded spontaneously to pre-recorded percussion sounds (Johnson 1987: 250; Whiteoak and Scott-Maxwell 2003: 269). In the same year, his compositions 'Rain on Water' and 'Kaffir Song', performed by the Don Burrows 4-tet (Sangster on drums) with the New Sydney Woodwind Quintet from the Sydney Symphony Orchestra at the Cell Block Theatre in Donald Westlake's 'Best of Both Worlds' concerts – raised the profile of modern jazz in Australia (Bisset 1987: 147).

He became increasingly active both performing and recording with members of the more progressive jazz community, including with his own groups. In 1967, he recorded on trumpet, vibes and various percussion in the John Sangster Group, Sydney on 20 and 22 February and 8 March, sessions which included contemporary pop material; on drums and vibes with guitarist George Golla on 14 July; on drums, vibes and percussion, he recorded 'Conjur Man' for the album *Jazz Australia*, commissioned by APRA;[15] he recorded with the Don Burrows Octet on vibes on 4 and 7 August

---

[15] Although this composition was attributed to Sangster, Clare asserts that 'Conjur Man' was actually by Bobby Gebert (Clare 1995: 125).

(Mitchell 1988: 57, 101 185). He also played with the Burrows group that year at the Expo 67 in Montreal and again at Japan's Expo 70 (Johnson 1987: 250). He continued to record with similar groups through 1968: on vibes with George Golla in Sydney on 23 October and with the Burrows 4-tet (no date), with pianist Col Nolan on 31 October (Mitchell 1988: 101, 154; Mitchell 1998: 43, 44).

Over the late 1960s, his work extended further into contemporary pop and fusion groups, including the band Nutwood Rug, then at Australia's first rock festival, 'Pilgrimage for Pop', at Ourimbah on Australia Day weekend, 24–25 January 1970, it appears that he presented a jazz-rock performance (Whiteoak and Scott-Maxwell, 2003: 277). He spent an extended period playing in the progressive rock band Tully as the house band for the rock/pop musical *Hair*,[16] and in late 1969 recorded the album *Ahead of Hair* (Festival FL-33,685, mono; SFL-933,685, Mitchell 1988: 185–6), and by 1969 he was further involved with the experimental counter-culture focused on the Ubu group, writing the music for Albie Thoms' film *Marinetti* (Clare 1995: 124–5). His work as a film music composer increased from the beginning of the 1970s. He often manifested an interest in the musical representation of the Australian landscape, as in the 1971 album *Australia and All That Jazz,* vol. 1, 1971, and vol. 2, 1976 (Mitchell 1988: 186,

---

[16]The Sydney production of *Hair* ran from 5 June 1969 to 10 March 1973 (Whiteoak and Scott-Maxwell 2003: 586 and 'Hair Australian Production' at http://www.ovrtur.com/production/2883,168 accessed 27 June 2023). Sangster claimed to have been with it for the full run, except for time off for the two Expos, Canada and Japan (Beilby interview 1994), but Montreal was in 1967, before the *Hair* production began, and Sangster reportedly left *Hair* in February (Lee 1970)

187) and now carried this over into film music, particularly in the Australian TV series *In the Wild with Harry Butler*, which ran from 1976 to 1981. He continued to record with various jazz groups,[17] but composition gradually became his major activity, particularly for film and, inspired by The Beatles, for recording (Bisset interview 1977). This was an extraordinarily prolific and wide-ranging stage of his career. Mentored in the fields by colleagues such as Geoff Kitchen, Bob 'Beetles' Young and Sven Libaek, he also began to study closely the work of Ellington and scores of Ravel, Stravinsky and Hindemith, and studied books on orchestration by Russ Garcia, Henry Mancini and Cecil Forsyth's *Orchestration* (Sangster 1988: 112–13). He

---

[17] See, up to the conclusion of *The Lord of the Rings* in 1977:

1971 – On vibes and numerous percussion, records with his own group, no date [nd] Sydney (Mitchell 1988: 186); on percussion records with Laurie Lewis, Sydney nd (Mitchell 1988: 134).

1972 – On vibes, with Len Barnard, 4 March (Mitchell 1988: 22).

1973 – John Sangster's Concert Orchestra; his instrument(s) not listed, Sydney nd (Mitchell 1988: 186); On vibes with George Golla, Sydney, around May (Mitchell 1988: 101); On vibes with Dave Dallwitz, Sydney, 24 August (Mitchell 1988: 74).

1974 – On vibes with Dave Dallwitz Melbourne, 9 March (Mitchell 1988: 75; Mitchell 1998, 68).

1975 – On percussion with Kerry Biddell, 'early 1975' (Mitchell 1998, 31); on vibes with Bob Barnard, November 3, 8 and 29 (Mitchell 1988: 16); on percussion with Billy Burton's Orchestra, Sydney nd (Mitchell 1988: 60).

1976 – *John Sangster and Friends*, on vibes, Sydney nd (Mitchell 1988: 187); on percussion with Col Nolan, Sydney nd (Mitchell 1988: 155); on vibes with Bob Barnard, 23 October, November (Mitchell 1988: 17); on vibes with Mileham Hayes, 3 November (Mitchell 1988: 13).

1977 – *Double Vibes: Hobbit* Swaggie S-1376 with Alan Lee, 16 April, Sydney (Mitchell 1988: 188); *For Leon Bismark*, on drums and xylophone, Sydney 3 July, 16 September (Mitchell 1988: 188).

began playing drums in TV studio orchestras, including the Bobby Limb Show. He composed and arranged extensively for film and television, often in projects that evoked the Australian landscape and fauna. Further work in this field included the animated US series called *The Funky Phantom*, produced for Hanna-Barbera Productions through the Australian Air Programs International (Sangster 1988: 180–3; for details of his work through this stage of his career, see Sangster 1988, 112–17, 172–9 188–9).[18] Len Barnard recalled:

> It was interesting to see him with his little click track and the film going through on a little thing, on a tiny little screen like that and he had a click track, and he had the click track all worked out, numbers and what he was going to put in there when that certain thing came up. So it was a long and laborious job and he did such a good job. And um I've never seen it myself, but apparently it's still going around the world, and doing bits [biz] here and Czechoslovak [inaudible] Brussells, and he's, I don't know if Petra's getting any royalties from it, I don't know. (Len Barnard interview 2003)

Such work helped to provide a financial base on which he could begin to build projects closer to his heart, in particular what became the multi-album *The Lord of the Rings*. In 1971, he and Bo moved out of the Cross to a house in Narrabeen (Sangster 1988: 131, 194), where he recalled in an interview with Roger Beilby that he lived for twenty-five years. This is impossible, as he died in 1995, only twenty-four years later, which included

---

[18] See further https://en.wikipedia.org/wiki/The_Funky_Phantom, accessed 27 June 2015),

residency in Queensland from 1992. This was also the year he recalls meeting sound engineer Martin Benge (Sangster 1988: 194), with whom he would begin a long association, including for *The Lord of the Rings*.

It was in 1973 that the first musical disclosure of his fascination with Tolkien's *Lord of the Rings* appeared, in the form of *The Hobbit Suite* (Mitchell 1988: 186), released on Swaggie S1340, a label originally founded by Graeme Bell, but by then owned by Nevill Sherburn, to whom Sangster had yielded all composer royalties (Sangster 1988: 195). The band, with Sangster on vibes and percussion, included what would be the main nucleus of the musicians who would go on to record *The Lord of the Rings* on EMI Records, the first double album volume of which was recorded over 19 and 20 August 1974 (Mitchell 1988: 187). This won the Australian Record Awards 'Jazz Award' and encouraged EMI to continue to commission additional volumes (Sangster 1988: 199).[19] It was followed by volume two in 1976, then volume three, as in all others, a double LP set, in 1977 (Mitchell 1988: 187–8; the catalogue numbers are, in order, EMC 2525-6, EMC2548/9, EMC2580/1). Although no longer under the rubric of the three-volume set (to which this monograph primarily confines itself), he was not finished with the subject, and in 1978 he released *Landscapes of Middle Earth*, EMI 2642 (Mitchell 1988: 188). Writing and recording *The Lord of the Rings* (including *The Hobbit Suite* and *Landscapes of Middle Earth*, took eight years, and by his own estimate, it came to

---

[19]Graham Lyall recalled it was *The Hobbit Suite* that 'did so well, it financed *The Lord of the Rings*. And that did so well it financed everything else' (Gould and Lyall Interview, 2003).

seven-and-a-half hours of music. He describes its incubation and progress in Sangster 1988: 198–9.

Sangster played vibes and percussion on all the recordings in the series, as well as on an album he recorded in August 1978 with pianist Tony Gould (Mitchell 1988: 103).[20] In April of the same year, he also recorded an album, the first on his own record label, Rain-Forest Records, based on the poetry of Edward Lear, *Uttered Nonsense* (Rain-Forest YPRX 1749/50), playing vibes and various percussion, including marimba and glockenspiel, Sydney, in around April (Mitchell 1988: 188–9).

Throughout this extraordinarily fecund period of recording activity, he was also busy performing live. In February 1978, he began a Friday night residency at the Old Push in a quartet with reed player John McCarthy, pianist Chris Taperell and drummer Laurie Thompson (Linehan 1981: [5]), and the following year rejoined Judy Bailey's group (Sangster 1988: 211). He recorded with pianist Tony Gould in 1978 (Mitchell 1988: 103), and the output of Rain-Forest Records continued with Sangster usually on vibes and various percussion. The second on his label was *Peaceful*, 1979, Rain-Forest YPRX1747 (Mitchell 1988: 189; although Sangster's album notes are dated 1979, the copyright year is 1980). This was followed also in 1980 by *Meditation* Rain-Forest RFLP-003 (Mitchell 1988: 189), and *It Don't Mean a Thing If It Ain't Got That Doo-Wup Doo-Wup Doo-Wup* Rain-Forest RFLP-004 (Mitchell 1988: 189).

---

[20] Sangster writes of the origins and evolution of his extended compositional oeuvres, including *The Lord of the Rings* suite; see Sangster 1988: 145, 146, 176, 194ff, 217, 231.

In late 1980 he recorded *Requiem (for a Loved One)* Rain-Forest RFLP-005, dedicated to Janice (Bo Diddley) Byrnes, 'and lost interest in quite a lot of things for a while' (Sangster 1988: 202). The two had been separated for up to a year before she died at the age of forty-three over the night of 2–3 June 1980, in Room 7 in the Crows Nest Hotel of acute alcoholic poisoning (Byrnes 1980). Appearing only about four months later, all ten compositions on *Requiem* are dedicated to her, and his 'headline' sleeve note reads: 'Sweet, she was, and lovely, and lively, and little. And dearly loved. Bo Diddley we called her and yes she met the real one, the black one, the big one after whom she was nicknamed; and he laughed and gave her a great hug. But she never got to Paris France'.

He continued recording into the early 1980s, including on 'handclaps' with the fusion band Crossfire in 1981, WEA 600112, 175129-2 (Mitchell 1998: 66), and in 1982 the album *Fluteman* Rain-Forest RFLP-006 (Mitchell 1998: 212–13), based on the music he had written for the film *The Fluteman* which had premiered on 26 October of the same year (see further Myers 1982). He recorded with Don Burrows sometime in 1982, then again in 1983 (Mitchell 1998: 44, 45). In his memoir of 1988, he had estimated his output at 205 'pieces of music composed, recorded and released … Almost twenty-two hours of it' (Sangster 1988: 225). Although his final recording appears to have been with Burrows in 1983, in his 1988 memoir he wrote, 'There are three more jazz albums recorded, mixed, and awaiting release, and a whole drawer-full of other scores ready to go. Suites and stuff' (Sangster 1988: 203). At about that time, he had evidently formed a relationship with a woman called Elizabeth (Sangster 1988: 256, 258), as indicated in the dedication of his memoir completed in 1987 and published in 1988: 'For Liz, who got me going again' (Sangster 1988: [xiii]), and who 'gave me a kick start' after an unproductive period of depression (Sangster 1988: 257). In 1987 he also referred to performing a song he wrote called 'Flowers for Elizabeth', 'a love song' (Sangster 1988: 255, 256).

In 1992, when he learned that he had cancer, he moved from Narrabeen to Brisbane, where he lived a 'very knockabout existence . . . and he was staying in some pub there in South Brisbane, . . . he sort of lived a very dissolute life' until he met Petra Schnese (b. in Berlin on 25 November 1944), who 'pulled him around, she got him around, smartened him up a bit' (Len Barnard interview 2003). The two took up residency as partners at 23 Manion Street, Red Hill. Notwithstanding John Clare's reference to her as Sangster's widow in a review of the album *The Last Will and Testament of John Sangster* (Clare 2002), they in fact never married, although after Sangster's death, she changed her name to Petra Schnese-Kleist-Sangster in honour of him and also of both her parents, Schnese-Kleist (Schnese 2015, personal communication to the author: 5 July). Petra was herself a musician, a member of a band that blended New Orleans and R&B styles (Beilby interview 1994), and this doubtless turned the ever-eclectic Sangster ear in a new direction, towards Country and Western. He performed at the Wangaratta Jazz and Blues Festival in October 1994, reviewed by Kevin Jones in the national newspaper *The Australian* (see also Jackson and Jackson 2022: 308). In September 1995, he played his final gig at the Noosa Jazz Party, and died of liver cancer the following month, on 26 October, with Petra at his side (Schnese 2015).

His final work eventually emerged after his death as the CD *The Last Will and Testament of John Sangster,* Move MD 3255. Len Barnard, who played drums on the CD, recalled:

> He had these things that he left, he was writing. He knew he was on borrowed time, you know, and he was writing stuff. And he envisaged a slightly larger band I think, you know? But we had a bit of a job. Tony's better on taking things [or?] transcribing things off arrangements than I am. So he did most of it. The arrangements that we had were reasonably sketchy, you know. So we made of them what we would. And I don't know – as I mentioned in the notes – I think John would have ap – they mightn't have been exactly the way he wanted it but I think that he would have approved that we had a go at it in that vein. So, uh, I still think that [laughs]. (Len Barnard interview 2003)

At his death, he left behind a nine-page list of around sixty compositions that he evidently had planned to record (Chamberlain 1996). Mark Wright reports that after Sangster's death, Petra sent him about twenty-four reels of tape, out-takes from various recording projects mainly associated with *Lord of the Rings* (Gould and Lyall interview 2003). In recognition of his service to the music, in 1988 John Sangster was elected to the Montsalvat Jazz Festival 'Roll of Honour'.

# PART II

# 3 Sangster
## The sensibility

## Introduction

The nature of the relationship between the artist and his work is a subject of perennial debate. Is the work to be considered as transcending the human being, the latter being irrelevant to an appreciation of the former? Or are the two inextricably entangled? Here, I simply state a position, the argument for which is for another place and time: Sangster's life and work are interdependent. This is particularly evident in an expressive form like jazz: fluid, performative and in permanent evolution even during the process of fixing the work as a permanent recording. Let us then first consider Sangster – his sensibility and temperament – although the distinction between the man and his music is provisional, simply a taxonomy within which to organize information. Because music was so central to his life, we shall often cross over into his work as a composer and performer, anticipating the next section of this commentary.

# Sonocentricity

In his memoir, Sangster wrote of the sound of the Japanese shakuhachi: 'I couldn't believe what I was hearing; the sound of it took me by the heart' (Sangster 1988: 168).

Sangster was obsessed with sound.

I intend the word 'sound' in its broadest sense. The case of a conventional written score makes the point. The precise intention of a score is to distinguish the music from noise. But Sangster's fascination with sound in its totality extinguished the distinction. For him, the division between culture and nature, music and noise, was fully permeable, whether it was the 'noise' of the natural world or human artefact.

The sounds of birds and animals were rich with musical potential. Working on a film based on a Judith Wright poem, 'The Blind Man', he seized on a reference to 'the cry of the Australian bush curlew. So I got hold of a recording of the bird and slowed his call down about twice, and then wrote it out for two alto-flutes and a string bass and used that as the basis for the film's music' (Sangster 1988: 172). Similarly, a project involving his dog Ralph, who had been:

trained to the headphones. I'd play certain music tapes through the phones at Ralph and she'd howl. Nathan's [Waks] dog sang for him too, when he played certain musics on the cello. The idea was to set up the two dogs in the studio, each with the appropriate sounds coming at them through their headphones, and record the two dogs' vocal reactions.

Then the fun would start. I'd write some music in and around the dog-music tracks for Nathan and me to play. And to improvise over, cello and vibes. Mix it all down and what've you got: When Dogs Bark, is it Music?' (Sangster 1988: 231)

Even language itself was as much a luxuriating in sound as a body of lexical meanings. Tony Gould reproduces examples of letters he received from Sangster. One of them signs off 'With all my best love, oo-roo, see ya chip Pertater. Sango' (Gould 2023: 99), exemplifying the letters' general rococo feel for the *sound* of language, which belongs in a tradition of aural orientation that can be found in writers such as Lewis Carroll, Spike Milligan, John Lennon, and Russell Hoban's novel *Riddley Walker*. It is not surprising that one of his late recording projects was the double album *Uttered Nonsense (The Owl and the Pussycat)* (Rain- Forest Records YPRX 1749/50) based on and interspersed with readings from Edward Lear's work, of which he wrote in the sleeve note that nonsense 'is very definitely not non-sense'.

The sound of objects simply colliding provided Sangster with inspiration. The composer Harry Partch constantly invented new instruments, 'But the nicest sounds of all, for me, come from his "Cloud Chamber Bowls": Pyrex chemical solution jars cut in half, suspended on a rack, and struck on the sides and tops with very soft mallets' (Sangster 1988: 232). That is, percussion, which became his preferred family of instruments, and indeed he received an Honorary Life Membership in the Percussion Society of Australia (Sangster 1988: 232), and his 'very favourite instrument of all' was the marimba (Sangster 1988: 138). He carried with him a hatbox of what he called his assorted 'percussion effects instruments', consisting of 'whistles and ratchets and car horns and gronkers and clonkers'

(Sangster 1988: 182). In performance he was increasingly attracted to experimentation with percussion devices, as at El Rocco, where he recalls playing timbales, chimes dipped in buckets of water, and rice bowls played with chopsticks, as well as a 30-inch Chinese cymbal: 'Once you got it primed up it would roar away like New Year's Eve in a Shanghai looney-bin' (Sangster 1988: 135). When Judy Bailey was playing, he would on occasions place ping-pong balls in the piano 'and things that went rattle and phoonk and squonch and blook when she least expected it' (Sangster 1988: 137).

In the pit orchestra for *Hair* he experimented with a range of sonic effects, including some which caused some alarm, but 'All I was doing was playing my percussion part, which said "Improvisation something Peaceful"' (Sangster 1988: 191). In Osaka for the 1970 Expo with Don Burrows' Septet, Graeme Lyall recalled that Sangster 'used to just spend all day in the pavilions, particularly the Mitsubishi pavilion, where they had these huge steel pipes, where you could hit with a hammer, and he'd just stay there all day hitting these pipes, cos he loved the sound of it' (Gould and Lyall interview 2003). At the Expo, he also heard an Indonesian gamelan orchestra. 'All those wonderful gongs and halves of vibraphones and things. Yet another brain-turning-around experience' (Sangster 1988: 170). He carried the same spirit into his recording projects, notably in the 'overture' to *The Lord of the Rings* and *The Hobbit Suite*. Recording what he calls a '"Magic Spell" for Gandalf the wizard', post lunch, 'and all musos know full well what that can mean', percussionist Ian Bloxsom 'somehow lost his equilibrium for a moment, and fell backwards into the tubular chimes, demolishing them nicely. It was a take, and happened right at the climax of Gandalf's "Magic Spell". We kept it in' (Sangster 1988: 176–7).[1]

Sangster's whole career is embroidered with 'Sonophilia', including during his early 1950s UK tour with the Bell band. In Hove, UK, he found a street full of mechanical chirruping birds and hurdy-gurdy machines: 'We would run down the footpath jamming pennies into each of these machines and stand at the top of the street hearing all this wondrous chirruping and whistling and tinkling' (Sangster 1988: 68). Under the stage in Southampton 'there was a clapped out mechanical piano with all the strings just hanging loose like bits of broken fencing-wire. But the penny-in-the-slot machinery still worked, and the piano would groan and clank out the most frightening, booming tremulous music. I loved it and played it endlessly until Mel, in desperation, jammed up the penny-hole' (Sangster 1988: 68).

## Eclecticism and eccentricity

Sangster's life and his aesthetics, the latter discussed in greater detail below, reflect a general career path that deviates, sometimes spectacularly, from the more general profile of those who emerged from the post-war traditional jazz movement in Australia. He was, in that sense, an eccentric

---

[1] There is no such track, thus entitled, on *The Lord of the Rings*. On *The Hobbit Suite,* there is a track called 'Gandalf the Whiz'. There is no concluding chaotic tintinnabulation on my version (Swaggie S 1340, 1973), where the ending is clean, tight and abrupt. Sangster's account perhaps betrays a retrospective wish that did not father the deed, but a 'wish' nonetheless.

sensibility. His domestic arrangements advertised the fact. Graeme Lyall recalled: 'Nobody was game to get there, cos it was a menagerie. He had every sort of animal known to the human race living on top of the El Rocco. . . . you walk in there and there's duck poo all over the floor, and – oh, it was terrible' (Gould and Lyall interview 2003). Narrabeen was a scene of similar disorder, both from my own recollection and that of Tony Gould (Gould and Lyall interview [2003]). At one point, Sangster owned what Graeme Lyall recalled was a three-wheeled Mazda:

> It was the smallest ute you've ever seen. It was like a – it had one wheel in the front, and two at the back, and it just fit his vibes on. And the gearbox used to seize all the time. So he always had a bottle of gin in the car, so it'd be one for him, one for the gearbox, and away he'd go! Somehow it used to free up the gearstick. (Gould and Lyall interview 2003)

His public life as a performer could be equally idiosyncratic. For a world satellite broadcast concert, Don Burrows instructed him: 'Don't be late. Don't be drunk'. Lyall continued:

> You know, we're on . . . world television, right round the world. So Sango rolls up, naturally out of it again, and Don, you know, really blasted him, so Sango just took off his jacket and put it on back to front, and walked up on stage and did the whole concert with his coat on backwards. So the whole world saw him with this terrible coat on backwards. Oh, dear oh dear. (Gould and Lyall interview 2003)

There is mischief here. Paralleling his eccentricity, Sangster was highly suspicious of what he regarded as any form of pretentiousness, or simply appearing to take oneself too seriously. This often manifested itself as iconoclastic pranksterism, a modern-day Till Eulenspiegel. Col Nolan tells the story of the Ray Price Quartet ending the night at Adams Tavern in George Street with 'The Saints', with John and reed player Pat Rose walking among the audience to start a conga line. On one evening, Sangster led the line out into the street, leaving only Nolan and Price in the Tavern. A considerable time later, Rose returned, reporting that Sangster had gone as far as Town Hall, where he hailed a cab and went home (Sharpe [2002]: 222–3). Col Nolan also recounted another occasion when it was Rose who was the victim. Playing at a lakeside school music camp with the Price quartet, Rose had taken out a canoe. Sangster paid some students to take boats out and ram him. In their enthusiasm 'they turn over Pat's canoe and he has to swim to shore. Poor old Pat. Here he is all bedraggled and we didn't know that he dyed his hair' (Sharpe [2002]: 228). He was both active and proxy prankster. At the Expo grand parade, watching organizer Robert Helpmann camping it up as he ordered an increasingly choleric regimental sergeant major around, Sangster and Ken Herron 'doubled up, fit to burst' (Sangster 1988:153). Similarly, he and fellow vibraphonist Alan Lee watched through a window of the Great Hall at Eltham as Brian Brown laboriously set up the stage and sound system for what they regarded as a pretentiously avant-garde performance. Lee and Sangster collapsed in schoolboy hilarity when, at the count-in, all the electrics spectacularly blew (Sangster 1988: 38).

There is a strong class dynamic at work in much of this. It is notable that Pat Rose was the picture of the dandified

English gentleman, with cravat, yachting jacket, immaculate white shirt, in Nolan's words, very much like actor David Niven. As in the case of my own experience playing with Sangster, I sense a mission to *épater les bourgeois*, and it complemented something very much like a *nostalgie de la boue*. He entertained bikies at his home in Narrabeen, and invited the garbos in for a drink, and loved mixing with wharfies (Gould and Lyall interview [2003]; Williams 1981: 71). To welcome saxophonist Keith Barr, newly arrived from UK, 'we took him to the nearby watering-hole for a bit of a welcome drink. A proper workers' pub it was, everyone in navy-blue singlets, stubbies and thongs' (Sangster 1988: 120); he chose the same pub ambience to prepare colleagues for recording sessions (see, for example, Gould and Lyall interview [2003]). On tour with Sven Libaek's orchestra, the string players sat in the front of the bus while what he called the 'riff-raff' (of whom he was a member) sat at the back. They stripped and poured beer over one of their group and:

> rolled him up in a tight little ball and bowled him down the centre aisle. So that he arrived, bollocky, up front amongst the straights. Touring-footy-team stuff. Heavens to Betsy, what a to-do. Shrieks of outrage. Great Christmas Humphreys! Hot towels for No 8! 'We're Artists, we are, how long to we have to put up with this? They're no better than animals, hoodlums, vandals, hooligans!' Guffaws from the low-lifers at the back. (Sangster 1988: 118)

The interpolation 'Touring-footy-team stuff' is of particular interest: Sangster was both a participant and a slightly cynical observer of such shenanigans. As John Clare shrewdly observed, Sangster's apparent contrariness was part of a 'naughty boy' persona (Clare and Brennan 1995: 126).

Part of that persona was an aggressive anti-pretentiousness, a conspicuous refusal to take things seriously. The case of music itself makes the point about a 'persona'. As we shall see in the next section, Sangster was meticulous as a composer/arranger. Yet, at the same time, he could affect an Ockerish heedlessness about music. Alan Lee once said to him '"You don't *play* the vibraphone Sangers, you play *with* it!" How right you are Spotters. It's only a toy, after all; nothing but a jumped up xylophone. Nice thing for having a good time on' (Sangster 1988: 220–1). This chimes with Tony Gould's observation that he was:

> Always smiling and fun, and you know, never – sort of mostly joyous and up, and never a serious conversation even about music, to be honest with you; cos he didn't see music as serious. I know that sounds ridiculous. But he just saw music as absolute bloody fun . . . That's all I think he saw it as. Despite the fact that he was a great musician. I don't think he ever took it seriously. Well he took music – he never took himself seriously. As far as I can tell. (Gould interview 2007)

Solemnity and institutional formality were anathema. He declined Don Burrows' invitation to participate in the newly established jazz studies course at the Conservatorium: 'I am one of those who believe that jazz can't be "taught" in any "school" except the hard-knocks one. You learn by doing' (Sangster 1988: 225). And 'doing' to him meant challenging rules, protocols, categories, engineering 'spontaneous' surprises.

All of this melds with his role as a cultural saboteur that has been evident in so many ways, and which was carried out with a great gift for manipulation. Keith Hounslow was alert to this: 'He was a weird man, boy, man. But very personable. That's why he got everyone in. He was really personable. *But I wonder at the use of that person* . . . he used people' (Hounslow interview 2007, my emphasis). The testimonies of his colleagues tell us, not that Sangster tried to force colleagues to do things, but that he was able to manipulate them to *want* to do things – a mark of effective leadership. To describe someone as 'manipulative' carries negative connotations, but I want to emphasize that manipulativeness itself is not a pathological aberration. Our entire survival requires us to discover how we might encourage – manipulate – others to behave as we would want them to. It is a daily negotiation between what we want and what we can achieve in social relations. 'Manipulation' of our environment is fundamental to harmonious social organization, absolutely necessary for growth and survival, and even civilization itself. It is practised daily by everyone, if we mean by 'manipulation' coming to understand how to work most effectively with other people to achieve our goals. There is nothing rebarbative necessarily implied in attributing manipulativeness to Sangster. He was simply highly skilled at it. Normally, we manipulate creatively within a framework of empathy for the other. And Sangster was a master at creative manipulation. Keith Hounslow said:

Oh, he was lovely, yeah, of course. He was drunk, and happy; he used to be good, happy, see? . . . . Lovely. Everyone loved working – and anything went. You know, he'd say, 'let's hear

that again' . . . [the music] was all scored, and they'd improvise
bits . . . And he'd be beaut, he'd see someone'd say 'I don't
think I played' – 'No,' he'd say, 'that was terrific!' You know, he
made everyone feel good. He was a good bandmaster, shall
we say, a record producer. . . John had command of the whole
recording session. (Hounslow interview 2007)

Tony Ansell also admired this skill:

His greatest attribute was the way he put people at ease in a
studio. And I don't think I ever struck anybody who could do
that as well as him . . . He was no fool, John. Quite the opposite –
a very smart man. You make people relax and then it comes out
naturally. He got a terrific result every time. (Sharpe [2002]: 224)

As in the transition from Hobbit to Orc, however, there was
a darker side to this, as Tony Gould, *inter alia*, noted:

But he also had a . . . very mischievous, destructive element about
him . . . He would . . . enjoy putting in front of a potential alcoholic,
a lot of alcohol. Like he turned [names a close colleague] into a
drunk . . . And John enjoyed that, because . . . any sign of weakness
in that department, John would exploit it. Cos he would figure,
well, it's your problem. And he'd stand back and watch [him].
There was a kind of slightly destructive element about that, and
he'd enjoy seeing somebody struggle . . . I mean my distinct
impression of – and several other people thought so too, at the
time – he would put [names colleague] in a dangerous situation
where he couldn't get out of – alcoholically . . . Any sign of that,
and he'd exploit it . . . A very complex man.

And 'he gave Don [Burrows] an awful time overseas. But Don's a
sort of arch-conservative, and also, John exploited that. He put

Don in a very embarrassing positions [*sic*] to see how he could get out of it' (Gould interview 2007). Much of the foregoing is interwoven with what has been called the Australian 'Tall Poppy syndrome', an inclination to diminish those who appear to be getting above themselves. This manifested itself indirectly in Sangster's robust advocacy of the local over the supposedly superior international product. He believed that Australian composers were capable of writing their own material rather than relying on US standards (Sangster 1988: 8). At the macro-level, this became a deep attachment to the principle that the local culture was unique and capable of standing on its own creative feet. Tony Gould considered that a pre-eminent characteristic of his work was its 'Australian identity' (Williams 1981: 71; see also Bisset 127, 166)), explicit in his two-volume *Australia and All That Jazz* albums (1971 Cherry Pie CPS-1008, L-70197; 1976 Cherry Pie CPF-1027, L70198), evoking Australian place, flora and fauna, in the same manner as his writing for the TV series *Harry Butler in the Wild*, and based on material written for the Australian Museum's Environmental Film Series.

His embrace of Australian vernacular culture suffuses the whole content and style of his memoir, to a large extent a string of matey pub anecdotes and held together by so much Australian vernacular that it is unlikely any non-Australian would be able to understand large swathes of it. Sometimes an entire paragraph is given over to larrikin Australianisms, having no bearing at all on the narrative. That is, the 'story' is subsumed to the construction of Aussie Ockerism. This generally benign chauvinism often betrayed a latent spirit of exclusion. When US saxophonist/educationalist Howie Smith arrived to take up the foundation Directorship of the new conservatorium jazz studies programme, Sangster recalled (and even the misspelling of Smith's name is a mild take-down of a foreigner and his institutional alignment): 'I liked Hughie Smith, but at the same time I felt a bit sorry for him. Round a dinner table with us Aussies he was like a fish out of water; being a Septic he missed most of the jokes, the rhyming slang. And when Deebs and George would start the old Pig-Latin, he was lost' (Sangster 1988: 227).

The reference to Deebs (Don Burrows) signals a much more localized model of his nationalism, in the construction of a social circle that amounted to vocational tribalism. Sangster developed a network of friends and musicians, a quasi-masonic community with its own mythology, argot and rituals, even to the extent that he felt the need to provide a five-page glossary in which various shared nicknames were 'translated' (Sangster 1988: 259–63). And, like one of his idols, Duke Ellington, he composed with these specific individuals in mind. As I enlarge upon below, a major aspect of Sangster's genius (in the original sense) was his ability to reconcile the pre-composed with the improvisational sensibility of his regular collaborators.In Gould's words, 'when he wrote and you went into the studio, you always felt that you could play that music and there wasn't anything that he hadn't – it was almost as if he wrote it for you' (Gould interview 2007).

# Alcohol

One of the essential bonds that held this masonic fraternity together was alcohol. It might seem indecorously intrusive to raise the question of a man's alcoholism in a discussion of his music, but Sangster himself gloried in his love of alcohol: 'I reckon that if God had meant for us to be teetotallers, He wouldn't have given us elbows' (Sangster 1988: 11). His memoir is swaggeringly (or staggeringly) drenched in booze. After recording an album with the Royal Australian Navy Band, he engages in a drinking contest with the service musicians, drinking in shifts until 3.00 am. He proudly remains the last man standing (Sangster 1988: 165–6). Chris Qua recalls:

> Sangster was a phenomenal bloody drinker – I couldn't keep up with him. Sometimes he would end up at my place on my couch – the couch of death. He had the constitution of an ox. He could drink solid, not eat a lot, lie down on the couch in a sort of batman position with the arms crossed on the chest, sleep for two hours, get up and do it all again, like nothing happened. (Sharpe [2002]: 227)

Graeme Lyall recalled that, when Sangster lived in Narrabeen, he 'used to just sit there and drink and hallucinate' (Gould and Lyall interview [2003]). At one point in his memoir, *apropos* nothing in particular, he interrupts his narrative to insert thirteen lines devoted to an inventory of drinking slang (Sangster 1988: 213).

Inevitably, alcohol became a vehicle of Sangster's pranksterism, sometimes maliciously so. Gould: 'I'm kind of lucky I didn't know John in those years – I might have ended up a drunk! He exploited any weakness one had for the firewater. Somehow he seemed to take great delight in other people's over indulgence' (Gould interview 2007). Sangster admits to being disappointed when a piper he hired for a recording project failed to fall into the 'trap' he had set up for him with a bottle of malt whisky in the recording studio (Sangster 1988: 59). And some unspoken backstory seems to lurk behind his almost off-hand recollection of Saratsina, one of his percussion mentors, whom he introduced to rum and coke: 'He got the taste something shocking . . . In only a few months he was dead. System wasn't used to it' (Sangster 1988: 131). Keith Hounslow was dismayed at the way in which Sangster used alcohol:

> I think he was evil. Sounds silly, and very strange to say, but he had a bad effect on so many people. With the grog . . . he'd have everyone over for weekends, and everyone'd get blind drunk . . . He'd be just smiling, 'have another drink!' and you know, all this stuff, and the few of them succumbed, and some people didn't get over it, I think. (Hounslow interview 2007)

As in the example of the backwards jacket recounted above, on occasion, Sangster sometimes 'prankstered' himself into a drunken indiscretion, as Tony Gould recalled: 'I think Sango got drunk one night at a governor general's do, and [Don] Burrows is Mr Prim and Proper – a wonderful man – and apparently Sir Rohan Cutler was walking down the aisle, and his crook leg, and Sango started going, boom, boom-boom [imitating a limping march]' (Gould interview 2007).[2] In spite of his stamina as a toper, in his later years, according to Hounslow, he himself

---

[2] Gould also reported, however, that Don Burrows told him 'I will never speak to John again. He lied in that book – about Cutler, the governor-general, doing the [limp, when the Burrows band was playing], you know?' (Gould interview 2007).

was increasingly likely to be impaired by alcohol (Hounslow interview 2007), until his life was blessed by the arrival of Petra, who was able to get him back on his feet.

All the foregoing events provide a cultural context and a temperamental profile that framed and shaped, in one way or another, his work as a performer, composer and studio director, culminating in his *magnum opus*, *The Lord of the Rings*. It is to this that we now turn.

# **4** Sangster
## The aesthetics, *The Lord of the Rings*

## Introduction: The 'pleasure principle'

There is an explicit continuity between Sangster's sensibility and his aesthetics. What I have referred to as 'sonophilia' seems to have been at the sensuous core of Sangster's temperament and more specifically the framework of his aesthetics. And his music was not situated in some semi-divine, autonomous realm, but designed to accessibly communicate with its audience. This was fundamental. 'If you don't communicate with the audience, you might as well stay home, because that's all music is – communication by the composer through the performer – to the audience' (Williams 1981: 57). 'I always give 'em none but the very best of Australian musicians to enjoy watching and listening to, lots of "talking-raves" during the concerts; not to explain or "edify", but just to make sure everybody knows we're having a good time and that it would be nice if they did too' (Sangster 1988: 219).

As a composer, his ultimate reference point was not some disembodied muse, but that of the listener:

In my mind I try to hear the band playing . . . First of all I hear
the tune and how the piece goes, then I pretend in my mind
that I'm sitting in front of the band, listening to them, watching
them play my music.

. . .

There is one thing I do that is a little way around writer's
block. I think, If I was playing a record of this, what would
I like the band to play next? And I try to write what I think
I would like to hear. . . . And I pretend in my mind that I'm
sitting in the audience listening to the band play this piece
and I make sure I am enjoying it. I make sure it is a good
rendition I am hearing, and just listen to what they play.
(Williams 1981: 54–55)

He practised music as a way of moving audiences, as a source
of affective engagement for all participants, 'the one-and-only
purpose of music is to make you feel good. Which includes
bawling your eyes out in the sad bits, which of course is
another way of feeling good' (Sangster 1988: 20–1). Tony Gould
confessed to the occasional put down of a fellow musician,

But Sangster, for instance sees good in everybody. At the
Myer Music Bowl when he was crowned King of Jazz and a
drummer from Melbourne and I were standing by, watching
some dreadful traditional band play, we were doing the
usual Melbourne thing of putting it down. And I went over to
John and said, 'What do you think of that?' And he said, 'Isn't
it wonderful? Look at him! Oh, yes, wonderful!' And it made
me realise that he sees the good in all those guys who play in
those trad bands, who are not very good but are having a nice
time. (Williams 1981: 73)

Without ever losing his affection for the early jazz tradition, Sangster's musical tastes and inspirations became extraordinarily broad. In his memoir of 1988, he still nominated as one of his three favourite recordings the Australian 'party' jazz album *Three Strings and a Dash,* EMI SOEX 9632 (Sangster 1988: 30).[1] It is a mark of the breadth of his horizons that the other two were Albert Ayler's *Spiritual Unity* and Louis Armstrong's *Potato Head Blues* (Sangster 1988: 161). Along with Charlie Munro, Sangster was one of the pioneers in non-Western experiments in Australian jazz, as in his 'Rain on Water', based on a Japanese scale (Bisset 1987: 147). In the words of Tony Gould:

> you've got this hugely broad vision of, you know, music, that's like, incredible. I've never known anybody that – he was hooked up with a country and western girl [Petra Schnese, later aka Petra Schnese-Kleist Sangster] for years – the last one, before he died . . . I said, 'what was it like?' and he said, 'oh, it was great!' He'd sit in the front row and listen to her play the banjo, or the guitar or something; he had no qualms about – it's just music. You know? That's all it is. (Gould interview 2007)

His musical career was thus marked by an ever-increasing, seemingly unlimited range of musical interests. He 'got tired of playing the same music all the time, which is why, coming out of the Bell band, I wound up playing with Don Burrows. At the same time I was playing with Ray Price, then there became

---

[1] Mick Fowler ukelele/drums; Wally Ledwidge guitar; Jack Craber bass, with Bob Barnard on some tracks; Fowler and Ledwidge are also the vocalists (Mitchell 1988: 205).

less and less of Ray and more of playing with Don' (Williams 1981: 56). And so it grew.In New York, he attended a Sun Ra performance:

> After the first piece I had to stumble outside and catch my breath; I was completely overwhelmed. My first really black BLACK music. What was it like? The Ellington band gone berserk? All I knew was that it was something I'd wanted to hear for a very long time; I didn't understand what it was all about but I felt completely at home in it somehow. (Sangster 1988: 158; his emphasis)

Likewise hearing Cecil Taylor: 'It was all played with stunningly brilliant technique, and with frightening intensity and fervour' (Sangster 1988: 159). In addition to Sun Ra and Taylor, he brought back from the United States recordings by Archie Shepp, Sonny Murray, Guiseppe Logan, Byron Allen, Albert Ayler, Mongo Santamaria 'and other Cuban and Spanish musics' (Sangster 1988: 161). On the way to Expo 67 in Montreal, with the Burrows band, he was deeply impressed when he heard a young John Handy (Sangster 1988: 150). He found a sense of liberation in all these experiences. Sitting in with Canadian musicians he found it 'a revelation . . . to play for the first time with a "free" rhythm section, where they didn't go one-two-three-four all the time and didn't invite everything into neat two and four and eight-bar blocks. A loosening of the bonds; I felt a great interior sigh of relief. Now I could *play*' (Sangster 1988: 151–2).[2]

----

[2]Whiteoak and Scott-Maxwell identify Sangster as an Australian pioneer from the 1960s in the use of electronic sound, of free jazz and collective total

His explorations took him beyond jazz. At the Montreal Expo, he discovered Iannis Xenakis, which led to Stockhausen (Sangster 1988: 155). He knew the work of Charles Ives (Gould interview 2007) and became drawn to David Lichine's ballet *Corrida*, Stravinsky's *Petrushka* and the work of Ravel. He began to study books on orchestration by Russell Garcia and Henry Mancini (Sangster 1988: 56, 95). Talking about people he'd played with, he recalled: 'I went out to Montsalvat and I played with Tony Gould, and he did one of his usual bodgy Mahler introductions' (Gould interview 2007). The irreverent reference to Mahler alerts us to a democratic spirit that invested his musical tastes. He found pleasure in all sounds and all musics. Tony Gould recalled, 'he had this attitudinal thing about music that wasn't in any sense elitist . . . I don't think I ever heard him make a critical comment about somebody making music' (Gould interview 2007). Sangster used to make Gould play 'Among My Souvenirs' and he listened to 'Sally' and all those ballads (Gould interview 2007). He found Percy Grainger's treatments of 'Danny Boy' and 'Love Walked In' 'heart-stopping, beautiful' and 'Almost unbearable it's so lovely' respectively (Sangster 1988: 228). He took great pleasure in hearing Nathan Waks playing the Guanieri cello with the Sydney String Quartet on *The Lord of the Rings*, but 'he loved everything about music and people. It wouldn't matter if they were a banjo player, he'd stand there and enjoy it' (Sangster 1988: 230; Gould interview 2007).

---

improvisation, of jazz-rock fusion and of non-Western musics (Whiteoak and Scott-Maxwell 2003: 249, 269, 277, 290, 380).

Although he journeyed so widely musically, there were inevitably some places he found more congenial than others, and those preferences are instructive in an attempt to construe Sangster's aesthetics. As *The Lord of the Rings* demonstrates, Sangster was drawn to 'programmatic' music, music that told a story or aroused emotions. And perhaps this is why he showed negligible interest in bop. He had little to say about the sub-genre in his memoir. He recalls playing in what he called Lyn Christie's 'Be-Bop Band', but his main comment is that the songs were taken at 'about ten thousand kph', and that he was afraid of 'flagging' (Sangster 1988: 144). His only other explicit reference is 'reading somewhere that Fats Waller used to decry the then-new jazz music. He would get upset and yell at the young cats who ventured too far out, "Stop that boppin' and a-stoppin', and play that jive like the rest of us guys"' (Sangster 1988: 227). There is no indication here of taking any particular pleasure in the style, and in his own work as a composer and bandleader, he pretty much leaps over bop, straight to freer post-bop forms. What these shared, but bop did not, were two characteristics that were important to Sangster. First, from Jelly Roll Morton to Sun Ra, they embraced collective improvisation. Second, bop is only 'about itself', for the most part a hermetically sealed exercise in 'pure' music. Even when a bop head is adapted from the 'great American songbook' repertoire, it generally sheds any referential luggage, as in the lyrics, to become an exercise in musical craft for its own sake. Sangster always showed a strong affinity with jazz that evoked something 'out there', that was a musical mediation of emotion, place and person. On *The Lord of the Rings*, these evocations are explained in his own cover notes. Other jazz areas that he explored, but ultimately found unappealing, included 'Fusions' (Sangster 1988: 229–30); he deployed strings in *The Lord of the Rings*, but had reservations about jazz/'classical' fusions (Sangster 1988: 230). And of the critically acclaimed 'Best of Both Worlds' Cell Block concerts, he recalled, 'All jolly good fun, but what's the point, I found myself thinking afterwards, on the way home' (Sangster 1988: 230).

The reference point around which he circled in *The Lord of the Rings* was what Crossfire's Mick Kenny called 'Cosmic Dixieland' (Sangster 1988: 217), and pre-bop sub-genres (see further Clare and Brennan 1995: 126):

> Reflecting on how 'the Popular Music of *my* day shared the same rhythms as my jazz music; the old dotted quavers feel. Ting ting-a ting. Swing. Mills Brothers, Tom Dorsey, Harry James, Duke Ellington, Andrews Sisters, the lot. And how in today's Popular Music *everything's* even quavers. Um-chunga. No ting-a ting. It all gets to sound like some endless "beguine" music; predictable, boring. No "lift". No "lilt". Not "the sound of surprise", as Whitney Balliett so perfectly describes jazz music'. (Sangster 1988: 230–1)

Everything we have seen about Sangster's temperamental and musical profile is suspicious of the fully 'predictable'; while he prepared his recording sessions with evident fastidiousness, it was in the nature of his music that he also had to prepare himself for 'the sound of surprise'. This can be traced back to that aspect of the jazz tradition which ran as a continuous thread throughout his entire career: the model of collective improvisation which underpinned the music's earliest forms. While recognizing that his early education in traditional jazz was often bigoted, forty years on he still found delight in those early jazz forms (Sangster 1988: 20, 26, 56). And central to that, and to subsequent styles that engaged his attention, was the creative potential in collective improvisation (Sangster 1988: 231). It is worth quoting at length the way in which he carried this practice into his later musical developments. During his more experimental performances at El Rocco, he would start off with what bassist George Thompson called a 'Scra':

> which is where everyone just had a bit of a general thrash around together with nothing much particular in mind. No 'Theme', no chord structure, no stated rhythmic pulse. No key signature. Flexing the old mind muscles, finding out how everyone else is feeling that night. Also a nice way of tuning up to each other, checking if your instrument is going to be friendly that night or not . . .
>
> To me, it was just a way to re-introduce into my 'Modern' jazz music a bit of the 'collective improvisation' of the 'Dixieland' front line, the interplay between clarinet, trumpet and trombone; the improvised ensemble. The thing I grew up with and loved, and still do. And which I miss in the more contemporary idioms.
>
> Sometimes these 'Scras' would develop of their own accord into some kind of ordered piece of music. Someone would find a theme. Another would develop it, a tempo and a key would arrive, as if 'out of thin air'. And away we'd go. (Sangster 1988: 143)

This is one of the most comprehensive statements by Sangster of his aesthetics, drawing together all the apparently diverse threads of his career as a musician. It draws a link between what appear to be disparate elements in his output as a composer and performer, and that link is collective improvisation and the reconciliation between form and spontaneity. In his sleeve notes for *The Hobbit Suite* recorded in 1973 (Swaggie S1340), he praised Bob Barnard and John McCarthy as 'absolute experts in one of the elements which I desperately miss in the more "modern" forms of jazz-music, viz. **collective** improvisation' (his emphasis). It underpins what I think is the hallmark of his sensibility: the trust he invested in his chosen musicians to find spontaneously the mood within which to improvise over his basic templates, the equivalent of saying: here is the basic form (say a blues structure); here is the 'affect', the mood, place or person I want to evoke – now go ahead.

To a much greater extent than other Australian (or other) jazz composers and arrangers, he trusted his colleagues to produce something which even he had not planned in detail, yet which embodied his intentions as a composer. Few, if any, musicians were able to find that fine point of balance, to which trust and personal knowledge were central. At one extreme lies the machine-like and emotionless precision of muzak. At the other, a shapeless incoherence of 'Free Jazz' at its least appealing. Drawing on the model of collective improvisation of early jazz forms, Sangster allowed form to emerge spontaneously out of sound.

## *Working methods*

Sangster began writing 'in earnest' during the El Rocco days, and many fragments 'later became transmogrified into various suites and things, like the Lord of the Rings and the Hobbit stuff' (Sangster 1988: 143).[3] By the time he began *The Lord of the Rings*, he was composing for recording rather than performance (Sangster 1988: 146), and indeed many of the pieces in that suite could not be performed, being created solely through studio technology, as in 'The Great Battle' (see below). Both in his persona and his domestic environment, Sangster presented, and even cultivated, an image of absent-minded eccentricity and untidiness. A parallel to this can be seen in his compositional practice as a form of creative sonic 'leakage', as environmental sounds merged into his writing. He believed he could not have written the albums *Peaceful* and *Meditation* 'outside the serenity of this lakeside environment' in Narrabeen (Sangster 1988: 239). He attributed some of the musical effects in *The Lord of the Rings* to that setting:

> you may have noticed that in all of that Lord of the Rings stuff, the first thing that I wrote here, [in Narrabeen] there is a lot of trombone and glissandi. I have often wondered whether it is because the ambulance depot, hospital and firehouse are all nearby; sounds like the variable pitch of the sirens can really shift things in your mind. Again, you see, my mentor has been the Duke of [*sic*] Ellington, with the sounds of his trains and his Harlem airshafts. (Williams 1981: 55)

By the time he came to write *The Lord of the Rings*, the initial stages of composition drew on an extensive mental archive of sounds:

---

[3] For his account of the origins and evolution of extended compositional oeuvres including *The Lord of the Rings* suite, see further Sangster 1988: 145, 146, 176, 194ff, 217, 231.

> And I don't put pencil to paper until I can hear nearly all the
> parts in my mind and then I go and write it down, which is the
> next part of the fun. The best part is hearing it first. I do very
> little revision if I have messed something up, could have done
> it better, I'd rather go on to another piece. (Williams 1981: 54)

Gradually, what developed in his mind grew in scale, until 'it wasn't just a little suite going on in my mind, but whole double albums of stuff. Four sides of recorded music, perhaps twenty or more pieces, all somehow connected, all wooshing around in there at once' (Sangster 1988: 146).

Yet, when it came to the serious stage of setting down his ideas, he was evidently able to seal himself off from whatever was going on around him, sketching his ideas wherever he found or made the space to do so. Graeme Lyall described Sangster's apartment above El Rocco:

> It was amazing. The walls – two walls of the room were covered
> with brown paper, and the other two walls were covered with
> manuscript paper. And any ideas he'd just write it on the
> brown paper, and any musical ideas, he'd just sketch it onto the
> manuscript paper, so he wouldn't forget it. So this whole room
> was just a mass of graffiti and musical quotes. That's how he
> remembered all the themes. (Gould and Lyall interview 2003)

In spite of his sensitivity to the total soundscape, when necessary, Sangster was able to block out all extraneous distractions and to focus meticulously on composition and arrangement: 'he'd write all those arrangements in the Narrabeen pub – I saw him do it . . . – and he'd get into the studio, and there wouldn't be a wrong note anywhere.

And a big orchestra . . . how can anybody do that?' (Gould interview 2007).

Notwithstanding this meticulous attention to detail, one of the most striking aspects of Sangster's musical sensibility was his openness to the unexpected. He welcomed the unplanned, aleatoric intervention. He was not dismayed by slight errors in execution by his musicians. 'I don't really mind mistakes. If they are on the players' part it sounds as though they are making the music up as they go along, sounds as if they are improvising' (Williams 1981: 54). According to Tony Gould, 'If you ever made a mistake in the studio, Sangster *loved* it' (Gould interview 2007). On more than one occasion, he intervened to preserve the audible human presence in music, as compared with the approach prevailing in 'classical' music recordings. On one recording session, the producer said that he would try to remove the sound of the bass player's fingers, to which Sangster objected: 'My dear man, that's a human being playing an instrument. Leave it alone' (Williams 1981: 72; see also Gould interview 2007). Tony Ansell recalled:

John was not a nit-picker. If there was a tiny error in there, and it didn't clash or go badly against the music, he'd leave it. He liked that. That would be anathema to some other people . . . But John wasn't like that. He liked naturalness in the music. In fact he booked one guitar player because he wasn't a perfect guitar player. He liked the fact that this guy sounded like it was a little bit too hard, you know. I don't know how to describe it. It was just that he wasn't that wonderful and John used to like that quality in his playing and that's why he would book him. (Sharpe [2002]: 224)

The respect for the 'human' sound in music was complementary to the importance he attached to the individual 'signature' in jazz performance. Two of his greatest musical 'heroes' were Maurice Ravel and Duke Ellington (Williams 1981: 54; Sangster 1988: 260). And the strength of the latter lay in his ability to write for individual musicians (Williams 1981: 55). In the words of Tony Ansell, 'he would very much write for particular players he had in mind. He knew exactly what each guy could do and he would book him for that' (Sharpe [2002]: 225). His collegial community was recruited because of their personal approach, rather than some depersonalized concept of virtuosity. 'Virtually all these larger "works" (plays' would be more like it) were composed with particular musicians in mind. Not only for the ensemble sounds I wanted, but it got to where I was hearing the specific 'kind' of improvisation I wanted from the soloists, and would instruct them accordingly in the studio' (Sangster 1988: 146). And having chosen them for that 'signature', he trusted them to play as they pleased. Tony Gould:

He always let you play the way you wanted to. So, whenever you got engaged to do a recording or something, there was never any question of saying 'I'd like you to do this or that'. . . . So he wrote music for all the people that he hired, that actually suited them, not suited him, but suited them. (Gould interview 2007)

In part, this was also because he chose sidemen with a history of shared tastes, enabling a masonic shorthand as he briefed them for a recording. Len Barnard was one who shared the 'codes':

He'll give me a drum part and over a passage for tom toms he'll have written *'The Mooche'*, so I'll play like on the Ellington of that tune. And he'll say 'Dave Tough on the last chorus of *Nobody's Sweetheart*, do you want to do some of that?' I'll say 'Oh yeah', and do a few things in the style of Dave Tough. (Williams 1981:19)

And if the musician were not versed in the relevant jazz lore, Sangster would give him guidance that left plenty of room for individual discretion. Speaking of the album *For Leon Bismark* (1977 Swaggie S1379), Sangster recounts:

This was written with two specific groups of players in mind. Bob Barnard does the Bix things, of course . . . I thought long and hard about the trombone parts, and, while there were at least a couple of players around who could do me more than passable 'Miff Mole', I decided on me mad mate Bob McIvor . . . He'd never heard of Bix. Or Miff Mole, for that matter. I told him just to play the written bits along with the others and when the improvisations came up, either solo with the ensembles, gimme some hot jazz and be more than a bit silly. He got the idea. (Sangster 1988: 200)[4]

If a shared, quasi-masonic culture created the conditions for effective musical collaboration in Sangster's projects, then alcohol was their lubricant. As we have seen, Sangster himself took a swaggering pride in the importance of booze in his life and work, even in live performance. Before starting a gig at El

<hr>

[4]See also the testimonies of Ed Gaston (Sharpe [2002]: 222); Don Burrows (Sangster 1988: 6); Tony Gould interview 2007; Chris Qua (Sharpe [2002]: 227).

Rocco, he made sure everyone was well-primed, as Graeme Lyall recalled:

> And every gig you'd meet at that pub across the road from the El Rocco . . . And the precursor to the first set was a double crème de menthe, double brandy, and soda, for the whole band. And if you got there early enough you got about two or three of them in. So we'd stagger back and stumble down the stairs, and he'd just hit the A 440 on the vibraphone. That was the first tune. It went from there, and the whole first set was based around that, and went for about 45 minutes. And then back to the pub again. (Gould and Lyall interview [2003])

## *Recording*

Sangster brought all these resources to the recording process: the imperative to communicate a narrative affectively, the assembly of a cohort of musicians whose work he knew and trusted, the establishment of a fine balance between design and creative space for his musicians, whose mood also required some 'engineering'. When Tony Gould arrived in the studio, 'there would always be a cartoon on the piano, something he knew I would think of as funny. And there would always be a letter or note, or perhaps a quote from someone, such as Edward Lear, that he thought I would like' (Williams 1981: 71). Even the deployment of alcohol became part of his 'design'. It wasn't just a supplement to recording but was part of the 'technology' of producing music. Describing his studio setup in his memoir, he tells us virtually nothing about such matters as equipment, mixing desk settings, placement of musicians, foldback – the 'technical' environment:

> Esky full of iced Foster tinnies in front of the front line, in case of snake-bite (we also carry the snake), the Dewars and lottsa Legal [ice] by the drum kit. Grants and Guinness side by side on top of the bass amplifier. And the 'Flytox' adorning the World-Famous Conductor's podium. It's an old Queensland drink, the 'Flytox', half Frigate UP rum and half Bitter Lemon. (Sangster 1988: 196)

Psychological ambience was given at least as much attention as recording technology. Tony Ansell:

> John had the most marvellous approach to recording and everybody loved playing for him. He had this calming influence . . . If you walked in four or five minutes late and were all nervous and up tight he'd say 'Go outside. There's bottle of scotch in that bag over there, go and have a swig . . . When you're relaxed come back in and then we'll do something'. (Sharpe [2002]: 224)

Tony Gould participated in the Edward Lear *Uttered Nonsense* album and recalled that before the sessions started Sangster gathered the musicians in the early opener, 'and have a couple of overproofs, and then you'd go back to the studio, and there'd be a fresh bottle of Haig'. And for lunch he laid on silver service (Gould and Lyall interview [2003]).

This 'creative manipulation' is most striking in the case of mouth organist Richard Brooks, as recounted by Tony Ansell. The ever-acoustically alert Sangster had noticed that Brooks had a distinctive laugh. He booked him ostensibly to record on the mouth organ, and Brooks arrived at the studio at 10.00 am as agreed. Sangster said that they wouldn't be ready to do the mouth organ until lunchtime, gave him some money and told him to wait in the pub across the road. Lunchtime arrived, and Brooks was joined by Sangster who, so to speak, topped him up,

> and when they came back John had ready this impossible sheet music to play. It was all carefully stage managed without Richard realising it. Richard went into the studio and they are rolling the tape and Richard, by this stage, was quite drunk. John says 'Your parts on the stand Richard'. When John saw the sheet music with this most ridiculous stuff on it, which he couldn't have played in a fit, he started laughing. And they taped this laugh because that's what John wanted. He had booked him for his laugh, Richard didn't have to play a note and that laugh appears on the record (laughs) I think that's great. Only John could have got away with that. (Sharpe [2002]: 225–6 [All punctuation *sic*])

Sangster possessed a gift for settling musicians in the often tense ambience of a recording session, recognizing the need for latitude to bring out the best in musicians who were working in a genre in which the unpredictable was definitive. Tony Gould remembered Sangster 'standing over the vibes, in the t-shirt and the peak hat chortling at everyone trying to get through these charts. And I'd say, "is that all right, John?" And he says, "lovely!" You know, "lovely – good on you, love, yeah, yeah". "Do you want me to do it again?" "No no, that's fine"' (Gould and Lyall interview [2003]).

For all his air of casual informality, his preparation for recording was meticulous, not simply in terms of what he presented to his musicians by way of arrangements, but also in preparing them psychologically. This is reflected in the account of Tony Gould, well experienced in recording, who found Sangster's effectiveness in the studio 'absolutely stunning, highly professional'. Gould wrote a piece for chamber orchestra, which he wanted Sangster to conduct. He sent Sangster the score and the two met the day before the session:

> He has already marked the times and cues and things on the score. The morning of the session came and this time he was very, very serious. It was a 9 am call and for the first twenty minutes, although the session had officially started, he was talking to the musicians, asking them if they wanted a cup of coffee, things like that. So by the time we actually came to making the record, everybody was feeling terrific. I would say he had never had a conducting lesson in his life, but he knew precisely what was in the score, all the changes in the strings – and some of the bits were a little bit complicated – and he was so fantastic that everybody had a lovely time. The string players obviously love him; he is just a joy to go into the studio for. (Williams 1981: 71)

Gould also participated in the Edward Lear album:

> We got there and nobody played anything, just sat around for twenty minutes or so, chatting. Then, before you knew where you were, you were playing, without him saying, 'Come along now, you've got to do this or that'. So many record producers start looking at their watches and fussing, but never John. It is

pure psychology, because he knows that recording sessions are a bit nerve-racking [*sic*]. (Williams 1981: 71)

## *The Lord of the Rings*

It was this extraordinary balance between attention to both musical and psychological dynamics that informed *The Lord of the Rings* project. Prolifically experienced in the recording studio, Len Barnard found that 'Recording with Sango was really really marvellous. It was so relaxed. And er a bit of drinking went on you know in the studio and er, lots of laughter and gags, they were a funny bunch of fellas. It was quite a largish orchestra at times' (Len Barnard interview, 2003). In fact, the 'orchestra' at times numbered over a dozen jazz musicians, plus a full string section.

Sangster's approach to directing a recording session was distinguished by a reconciliation of the planned and unplanned. To a great extent, he mapped out the music beforehand, and for *The Lord of the Rings*, that 'mapping' included several unorthodox procedures. Graeme Lyall recalled that the suite was 'completely composed', but the individual pieces were simply numbered, without a title, and Sangster 'basically gave a brief outline, but not too much because he didn't want people to try to do something which they wouldn't normally do'.

He just wanted you to play. And the good thing about it – like, somebody said to me the other day, 'it's so tight', and that's not what Sango was about. If it was tight he probably wouldn't accept it. He just – if the spirit of the music was there, if it was take one, and there were mistakes, but if the spirit was there, that's it! You're not doing it again; I love that bit. You know. (Gould and Lyall interview [2003])

This chimes with Len Barnard's account:

John used to get up, and before each one he'd say, er 'This is a piece about so and so. Don't knock yourselves about too much, it's going to be rather gentle for a while, so if you take a solo in it, don't go over the top', just, er, just little things like that. He knew exactly what he wanted.

And what he wanted was an elusive balance between what he visualized/audialized for the piece and the freedom of improvising jazz musicians whose work he trusted. Len Barnard provided the most detailed accounts of how Sangster directed *The Lord of the Rings* recording sessions:

And the charts were always um pretty accurate. Well the framework was all done. Some of it was completely written out. The jazz solos were improvised because he would just say 'Play here, do your own thing there, etcetera'. But the ensemble passages and the framework of the piece, the arrangement as such, would be played off the charts. Although you had to watch yourself because he never used to do the orthodox things like having a – instead of having an 8 bar section, he'd have 7 [laughs] and then he'd go onto the next bit. And you know how your brain always works in 4 and 8 and 16, and then there'd be a 16 bar section which would be 17. And you just couldn't rely on chopping off what you were doing at the usual place because it was just a little bit different. Now this didn't happen all the time but a lot of times. And his writing was extremely accurate and he used to write in pencil on a score sheet, in a pub or anywhere. All the time he had . . . this big leather bag full of stuff – cigarettes, bottles of rum and um score paper and thousands of pencils and things. He used to scribble the arrangements out as he heard them, and when we got the – handed out the arrangements in the studio there was never anything to be altered. He might tack a bit on but he wouldn't alter anything, he'd [just say?] I might do something and put another coda on there. (Len Barnard interview 2003)

During the sessions, Sangster kept the tapes running continuously and would mine them for material that became part of the final suite. 'Longbottom Leaf' opens with a slightly stilted 'Spanish tinged' piano rag. The chorus is interrupted by laughter, stopping abruptly with a voice suggesting they start again. Further laughter, the piano continues but makes mistakes accompanied by more laughter. A two-note figure on bass clarinet stops amid further laughter. The music resumes with the two-note punctuation now from two reeds in harmony, then a break, as one reed comes to the fore. The piano then plays an up-tempo theme reminiscent of early Jelly Roll Morton, going in and out of tempo with different themes and styles such as stride. After an abrupt stop, the piano returns to the opening, amid further laughter. It stops for a discussion of the changes, resumes, accompanied by occasional laughter. Finally, it stops as though finished, resumes awkwardly with odd tempo displacements and missed notes, then ends. A similar sense of 'offcuts' pervades 'Goodnight', a collage of instrumental noodling including fragments of other songs from the suite. It has the sound of a free-for-all unwinding after all the stresses of the many and extended recordings so far undertaken. In Sangster's words from the cover notes, 'after all the "serious" music is done, when you know you don't have to play "proper" any more, and can relax and muck-up'. The track concludes by fading on a lengthy percussion section on assorted instruments like chimes.

A notable example of such a collage is 'The Great Battle', the production of which was recalled by Len Barnard:

> Everything that went on in the studio, sometimes a bit of, banter, or a few laughs or stuff going on between the brass section and the reeds, used to keep all that, and you'd hear little flashes of it being . . . interpolated, in some of the pieces where there was heavy stuff going on, like the great battle. And the great battle was just a big er [?] like a put together melange of all the stuff from various other tracks on the record, and he's put it on a . . . overlaid things, you know, until it got, ah, it starts off very softly, and there's a gathering feeling of conflict, and stuff going on [laughs] and shouting and little bits of laughter . . . you know the track, 'The Great Battle'. And then it disappears, it goes, as if they've just gone over the top of a hill, and it just goes away and disappears. (Len Barnard interview 2003; see also Gould and Lyall interview 2003)

It is a sound montage, including fragments from other tracks, sometimes at different speeds, mingled with random instrumental, vocal and other sounds: beginning with slowed-down extracts from the rallying 'Uncle Gandalph Needs You', gradually descending into acoustic chaos, subsiding after six minutes into an uneasy silence. In a mirror-image emotional mode, 'V-M-E Day (a Mondorian Phantasmagoria)' is 'A joyous cacophony' (Sangster's cover note), celebrating the victory over the 'Powers of Darkness', with instrumental, vocal and other random noises, fragments of melody, occasionally fleetingly recognizable.

Such tracks exemplify the extent to which his directorial activity is rooted directly in personal and musical experience rather than some theory-based agenda. And that experience incorporated personal memory. 'The music for *Lord of the Rings* is all out of my memory, my memory of how musics went … All that autobiographical stuff – which is what *Lord of the Rings* is – was things I had enjoyed during my life, listening to and playing jazz music' (Williams 1981: 54). As such, *The Lord of the Rings* reached back to his abiding affection for traditionally oriented jazz genres. As Len Barnard pointed out, 'it could be almost . . . autobiographical about John's musical loves over the years . . . he used to love Lu Watters and those recruiting marches like "Uncle Gandalph Needs You" and all that stuff . . . a sort of a crystallisation of all the things that had gone before' (Len Barnard interview, 2003). 'Uncle Gandalph Needs You' is a march with a 'strut' that easily transitions to dixieland. Similarly, 'The O'Goblin Tattoo' opens with drums and parade marshall's whistle. Trombone and bass trombone in low-register figures introduce a theme stated on trumpets, then joined by John McCarthy's clarinet playing free over the top, imparting a dixieland feel, harmonically reminiscent of 'Bourbon Street Parade', a reminder of how easily street march evolves into jazz. What follows are sections alternating between minor (recalling the feel of King Oliver's 'King of the Zulus') and major before reverting to the dixieland 'Bourbon Street' theme, before returning to the original theme. 'Tom Bombadil' also opens with a rollicking two-beat march and a transition to a minor theme with double trumpet breaks recalling Oliver and Armstrong, a two-trumpet break virtually a quote from their 1923 'Snake Rag'. 'Blues for Denethor' draws on another facet of the New Orleans marching band tradition, the funeral march, majestic, hymnal, gradually running through brief substitutions and key changes as the voicing becomes richer and more declamatory.

Len Barnard's reference to 'a crystallisation of all the things that had gone before' opens up a panorama of Sangster's influences. *The Lord of the Rings* draws on a broad spectrum of the ragtime/jazz/carnival/circus/vaudeville tradition, through not only dixieland, but also to much later and more radical aspects of the jazz tradition, including atonality, as in the mysterious, other-worldly opening of 'Ringbearer', a sonic fog which swirls over the ensuing theme played on horns and vibes. Elsewhere, he reaches back to a mode of Edwardian elegance. Some of his pieces with strings, such as the genteel ragtime-inflected openings of 'Elvish Dance', 'Elvish Tea-Party with Dance' and 'Three Is Company' suggest the pump-room-at-Bath or Dennis Wilson's theme for the late 1970s series *Fawlty Towers* (post-dating the beginning of *The Lord of the Rings* project). Sometimes Sangster draws on these period-flavoured pieces only to reshape them in unexpected ways, as in 'The Sweetness and Light Rag', opening with an ambiguous tempo, the clarinet implying a ballad, but then an underlying doubling up. He used other Edwardian forms, sharing with ragtime the use of several sections, but sometimes with the transitions between them less formally defined. As well as the frequent key changes characteristic of ragtime, he uses transitions of tempo, instrumentation, genre and mood. 'Bilbo's Birthday Party' opens with a part orchestral ragtime theme, passing through two parts to a brief string bridge to a third theme, then to a fourth, in which Bob Barnard's trumpet takes the lead playing a looser rhythm. Much of the character here, as in other tracks, is the tight formality of the orchestral backing against Barnard's understated rhythmic and tonal variations. The use of unexpected sonic contrasts is also striking in 'The Uruk-Hai', with Basie-style voicings over an aural nightmare of animal noises, giving way to a clear-air Buchanan solo over bass, and later, McIvor generating growing hysteria on trombone.

Many of his songs were new wine in the old bottles of established harmonic changes, a practice so widespread that it has its own name: contrafacts. The blues form is, unsurprisingly, a staple, but always refreshed either by Sangster's modifications or the creative vigour of the soloists. 'Beware the Barrow-Wight' is a variation of a blues form, opening with honky-tonk piano and John McCarthy. There is much use of dissonance as the backing enters, the mood deepening into an increasingly formless darkness, until reverting to a dark honky-tonk conclusion fading into auditory chaos. Similarly, 'The Balrog' is a variation on a blues; emerging from an acoustic cloud punctuated with monstrous growls, sounding like a herd of cattle; a theme emerges, in a menacingly low register on trombone and two baritones, reminiscent of a darker version of Milt Jackson's 'Bag's Groove', a blues that seems to hover between major and minor. Continuing background beastly punctuations which finally overwhelm the theme, which reappears up-tempo though over the same throbbing beat as the opening. Out of this chaos, with the rhythm maintaining the same pulse except for intervals at double time, emerges a Bob Bertles alto solo framed still by the acoustic mayhem, which gives way to a McIvor solo, again with a variable tempo background. McIvor is often dissonant ('a bit silly'?), then the horns subside back into a version of the theme until the music collapses into a low-register heap.

Contrafacts abound, tracks that are straightforward performances based on clearly defined original themes but over standard changes are brought to life by the quality of the soloists. The chord sequence for 'Arwen's Regret' is based on 'Moonglow', with passing references to 'You Ought to Be in Pictures'. 'Oliphants' harmonically recalls 'Exactly Like You', and you could play the melody of the standard '[When We Danced at the] Mardi Gras' over the changes for 'Rivendell Rort'. Sangster also adapted the harmonic structures of such standards as 'I Wish I Could Shimmy Like My Sister Kate' in the shimmering 'Vale Theoden'. The opening of 'Ithildin' recalls 'Mean to Me' and 'Making Whoopee'. After the opening of 'Thank You Perfessor', the song becomes a jaunty extroverted stride exercise in the style of 1950s Ellington, over the chords of 'Perdido' which Sangster gradually reassembles with the disconcerting logic of an Escher drawing, with tuned percussion punctuations and laughter. There is an orchestrated section with angular, sometimes whole-tone substitutions, and melodic passages reminiscent of other songs, including a reference to Joe Sullivan's 'Little Rock Getaway'. Sangster's vibes gradually assume the major lead, with a sax solo recalling the abandonment of Paul Gonsalves' famous 1956 Newport Festival solo on 'Diminuendo and Crescendo in Blue'. There are fully orchestrated exchanges between sections, with drum fills, concluding with a massive chord, chimes and laughter.

There is nothing nugatory implied in discovering 'intertextuality' in music. T. S. Eliot observed, 'Immature poets imitate; mature poets steal'. The most venerated symphonic and 'classical' composers are admired for the way they could incorporate tradition into their work, often in the form of folk material, from Liszt to Stravinsky. As in their case, Sangster's 'borrowing' was always refreshed by some unexpected twist and the personal voices of the soloists. 'Farewell Lothrian' is largely the same harmonic structure as Sidney Bechet's 'A moi de payer', played not as a waltz modulating to 4/4, but opening as a slow, funereal march. It then transitions to a major key, and rather disconcertingly includes a seven-bar theme, followed by a switch to a tango tempo, leading to a slow, declamatory conclusion with long reverb. Sangster's mental musical archive also reached beyond the popular music tradition to refer, consciously or not, to Paul Dukas' *The Sorcerer's Apprentice* in 'Legolas: Elf'.

Dissonance is a frequently used device, as in 'The Mirror of Galadriel', which opens with a two-note motif, then is overlaid with a descending line of soft chimes. Joined by a simple clarinet motif using either very heavy reverb or delay; then in the same tranquil mood, it transitions to a blues, with a further high register clarinet entering in a competing key almost as though overheard from the next room. The form then dissolves into free dissonance in which the clarinet takes on the sound of bird calls, intermingling with the vibes and low-register turbulence. It concludes with a drift back to the opening consonance. Most frequently, however, Sangster uses dissonance in the presentation of the darker side of Middle Earth. 'Frodo's Fantasy' opens with a tidy thirty-two-bar theme over familiar chord sequences but gradually melts into an atmospheric, formless 'fog' that opened 'Ringbearer', with rising unearthly dissonant wind, percussion and pizzicato punctuations. More nightmarish are 'Shelob's Lair', and 'Phantasmagoria for Moria'. The former evokes a pursuit through dark spider-filled tunnels, with sinister percussion phrases, formless and dissonant, gradually spinning into an almost amorphous statement from Buchanan on bass clarinet. The latter opens with two up-tempo blues piano choruses, then the entry of a trombone riff, interspersed with dissonant roars, which are sustained through reed and trumpet solos, and concludes in a kind of shapeless exhaustion. The same acoustic nightmares inform 'Nazgul' with its relentless threatening figure evoking fearsome winged aerial creatures. And an ominous low-register woodwind cyclic figure, joined by brass overlay, then dissonant saxophone 'squalls', with percussion punctuations. And the climactic horror is the 'Orcs', with menacing low-register brass, transitioning to Sangster on marimba in often dissonant free form, alternating with an aggressive, urgent brass figure, underpinned by brass punctuations sounding like cattle, rising to hysteria.

As implied by the foregoing, *The Lord of the Rings* is also marked by frequent radical stylistic transitions that are often encompassed within individual pieces, ranging from baroque and classical to structured jazz themes drawn from the earliest to the most recent (and often foreshadowing future) developments. This wide-ranging eclecticism extends to variations often incorporating various forms of Latin-derived rhythms. 'Merry-go-round' opens with a rhythmic pattern set up by hand percussion, which seems to foreshadow, then resolves into, a medium samba. 'Celeborn Celbrant' is also a melodically strong, ebullient samba, opening with percussion and vocal whoops. 'Hoblyti-Hoblyta' opens and closes on the 'Charleston' phrase that is based ultimately on the Cuban tresillo, the defining rhythmic unit of so much Latin music, often known as habanera (dance of Havana).

Although he had experimented with free form during his El Rocco days, Sangster became increasingly suspicious of its tendency towards undisciplined over-indulgence. Nonetheless, he occasionally exploited its influence in *The Lord of the Rings*. 'Goldberry' opens with a simple three-note motif on recorder, then underpinned by other horns before breaking into various forms of percussion reminiscent of tranquil oriental sounds. This is followed by a variation on the opening motif with horns, gently moving into improvisations suggestive of a minor blues, moving again via a gong to an orchestral development of the opening motif, including a baroque feel emphasized by Errol Buddle's use of oboe, then to a sumptuously backed trumpet/flugelhorn transitional passage and finally back to a variation on the opening motif, followed by further flugel improvisations. The use of simple figures in a context of asymmetries is further developed in 'Encore Gandalph'. After a declamatory, formally shaped fanfare opening comes, unexpectedly, unearthly clarinet figures over the bass, punctuations with a two-note figure on trumpets, a 'bridge' involving a four-bar exchange between sinuous soprano and trumpet follows, before returning to the 'A' section. A section of two-bar chases between reeds and trumpets is followed by a coda. The two-note figure returns in a different key on trombones, followed again a ghost-like clarinet. The bridge consists of exchanges between trombone (two bars), tenor (two bars), trombone (one bar) and tenor (one bar). The same two-note based theme with a turbulent bridge becomes the basic form of the composition, with variations in instruments and voicings, ending with a coda followed by a brief tumble into acoustic disorder.

As in these cases, Sangster is highly sensitive to the possibilities of aural contrast, both between instrumental voices and a dynamic range from silence to stridency. 'Galadriel' includes wide instrumental timbral and pitch intervals between brass bass and what sounds like a piccolo and exploits multi-themed, time-signature changes, and changes of musical mood from the gently lyrical to circus bombast. 'Three Cheers for Smeagol' is in three sections. It opens with walking bass and drums, moves to a theme on vibes with a minor feel, then is joined by low-register reeds in harmony, which is disrupted, followed by vibes as the tempo increases and the form becomes loose, with many instrumental sounds stacked up into a free collectivization out of tempo. The walking bass re-emerges and the theme is restated until the cello enters, floating in increasingly free form over the rhythm section, joined gradually by other voices again dissolving into free form until again the walking bass re-emerges from the chaos. Tony Buchanan then reasserts the theme on bass clarinet, and there is then another descent into sonic chaos, from which, once more, the bass emerges, and the theme is restated with dissonant interjections, finishing with a tight, orderly tresillo phrase. 'Hairy Foolish Shoeless Feet' also exploits various forms of asymmetry. It opens with group whistling, an instrumental passage accompanied by a lone whistler, then moves into a rapid-fire theme with a disorientingly ambiguous sense of form. The whistlers return in an exchange with instrumental punctuation, playing off contrasts between a steady ground beat and rapid-fire section and solo passages from Graeme Lyall.

But more often, as a composer/arranger, melodically and harmonically he preferred a symmetrical formal framework, drawing in particular on the full range of pre- and post-bop styles, including powerfully driving swing passages drawing on the big-band sounds of the 1930s to the 1950s. The suite opens with 'Off to Adventures', ajaunty, genial swing with several themes, drawing on standard turnarounds with shades of Basie and Ellington in the orchestration. The same influences are audible in 'Gandalph the White', 'Sam the Man', 'The Ride of the Rohirrim' and 'The Glittering Caves' which, after a statement in waltz time and a slow AABA trombone passage and a march section, ease into a more swing-like mode. In some of his slower ballads, such as 'Lullaby in Lorien' and 'Fair Eowyn', we again hear the spirit of 1950s lush Ellington. So too in the blues-based opening theme 'The Misty Mountains', which is followed by a declamatory passage introducing a new chorus that then leads to a bridging section that passes into minor passages with dissonant episodes before returning to a bridge and final theme, again with major/minor transitions. This is one of the most complexly underpinned of all the compositions. All these imply a form of pastiche, but he gives the work new life through a range of approaches, including using ambiguities and 'false scent' in terms of harmonic progressions and tempi, particularly arresting on the ambiguous tempos of 'Eleventy-One Today' (and in which Don Burrows' solo fades out with a reference to 'Swinging Shepherd Blues', the 1958 hit for Canadian flautist Moe Koffman).

For all Sangster's eclectic ventures into such effects as free jazz, sound montage, intertextuality, fundamentally he was a melodist, capable of composing or creating a context for the most memorable, clearly defined themes, yet which could still take unexpected directions, as in the jaunty 'Proper Fourteen-Twenty'. It is his attachment to form and melody that produces the most memorably beautiful moments in the suite. 'The Grey Havens' (misspelt on the CD cover as 'Heavens') has a stately largo feel, with sustained opening notes from the string quartet, with a serene eight-note marimba figure and sounds of (sea?)birds, joined by a meditative sax line in dialogue with vibes and woodwinds. This is among the most performed of the songs in the suite and was a particular favourite of Lyall's: 'all he told us was the king's body's put on this raft, and it just floats out to – on the lake, into the grey mists, and disappears. It's a really beautiful, descriptive piece of music. It's one of my favourites'; Lyall was equally enchanted by 'Blues for Boromir', 'another gem' (Gould and Lyall interview [2003]). Melancholy figures give way to a finely shaped five-note funereal theme swapped between two plunger-muted trumpets, swelling to a bluesy bridge recalling Nelson Riddle theme music from an urban elegy like *The Naked City* or *The Untouchables*. It is emotionally intense, with extensive use of dynamics.

Sangster himself was moved by a passage in 'Ants and Entwives'. Walking trees, a menacing low-register opening with almost human wails, all wooden instruments played by Sangster; a cello solo overlaid by percussion and indistinct vocalizing. There are occasionally recognizable thematic fragments, constantly interrupted or overlaid by indistinct phrases, sounds and punctuations. It is disturbingly, atmospherically dissonant. But for Sangster, 'I wrote the theme for cello and bass-clarinet, and then asked Nathan [Waks] to do me a sad, yearning-type improvisation over the top, for the long-lost "Entwives". Someone played me the record the other day, some thirteen years afterwards. Still gets me. Unutterably sad' (Sangster 1988: 231).

Since we are listing some favourite pieces, by way of concluding summary, I spend some time on my own, the piece that to me most succinctly encapsulates Sangster's 'genius'. 'Vale Theoden' is a requiem for the slain King Theoden as his body is borne from the battlefield. On chords adapted from the unlikely and rather banal source of 'I Wish I Could Shimmy Like My Sister Kate', a measured first chorus of simple crotchet chords on keyboard is followed by the entry of McCarthy on clarinet, with a relatively simple low- to mid-register improvisation. He is then joined by bass and sustained background strings as the clarinet rises in register in an emotionally dramatic use of silence and simplicity. In the next chorus, he is joined by Bob Barnard on trumpet, with equal respect for silence, economy and space. Then comes the entry of trombone (sounds like Bob McIvor) in a simple six-note repeated phrase slightly modified according to the changes. McCarthy is now in poignant upper register, and then all three horns rise in register, Barnard has now picked up the trombone figure, so that it has virtually become the theme, with McCarthy embellishing. McCarthy and Barnard continue upward, both now straining at the limits of their instruments, and occasionally even cracking notes. Finally, the trumpet drops out, and, with occasional trombone punctuation,

McCarthy returns to the fore, at the upper limits of the clarinet, and as the track fades at the end of the chorus, we hear briefly an intimation of even more intensity coming from McCarthy. It is one of the marvels of this track that this promise remains unfulfilled as it fades to silence, as though the intensity has now become too much; there is yet more mourning and grief, but it is too unbearable. According to McCarthy's recollection during a conversation referred to below, the decision to fade at this point was Sangster's, an extraordinarily bold decision given the promise of further to come in McCarthy's final fade-out, but all the more poignant for the grief being implied but not sounded. The affective power of this track is deepened by the steady slow march pace of the backing as a foil to the anguish of the horns, and in particular of McCarthy. Johnny McCarthy and I co-led a quintet for an extended residency in the Soup Plus jazz venue in the 1980s, and not long after I had bought a copy of this volume of the suite, during a break I told him that I thought that his particular work on this track was the finest I had ever heard him play. McCarthy, not normally a demonstrative man, was deeply appreciative, and said that of all the music he had recorded, he was most proud of this track. In my view, it is one of a handful of the most moving pieces of music ever recorded by any jazz group anywhere. One of the most important dynamics in collective improvisation is trust. Nothing Sangster has ever produced more convincingly demonstrates his gift for bringing together composed material with musicians he could so trust as to stand back and allow them to complete it with such magisterial authority and empathy.

# Coda

When *The Lord of the Rings* project was completed, Sangster simply moved on. Len Barnard recalled, 'I don't know what happened to the charts, I really don't know. I didn't, I couldn't see that he would shred them. But I think he tossed them away somehow, because he said, er, "The beast is slain. It's dead now, I've done it. That's done. So I've started to move on to something else"' (Len Barnard interview, 2003).

As a concluding tribute, I provide the following appreciation from Tony Gould:

my feeling is that the influence he's had on people – a lot of people – is profound. And that's almost more important than the music, in the end. Cos I was absolutely taken with John, and his attitude to music, and I know Len, and not so much Bob, but all those boys like Laurie Thompson, and all those boys, they tell you the same thing: he had this kind of – I don't know what it was – this aura about him that, you know, when you were making music with him it was the best thing you ever did in your whole life. . . . Everybody loved him. We never went home. Twelve o'clock and we were still in the recording studio listening and joking and laughing and drinking and stuff. It was most amazing. I've never struck that with anybody else before. Not even close, you know? And Lyall will tell you the same thing, you know? A most amazing man. I still miss him, to be honest. I'd kill to play with him again. That amazing sort of freedom of knowing that whatever you do is going to be all right. (Tony Gould interview 2007)

# References

## Primary sources

Bell Papers. Private papers, Graeme Bell, Mitchell Library, Sydney NSW, Bell Box 4, BELL ML 1771/93, 4 (34).

Byrnes, Janice. 1980. Death certificate.

Chamberlain, Anne. 1996. John Sangster: Unrecorded Brisbane Works 1993-1995.

Decree Absolute for the dissolution of the marriage between Shirley and John Sangster, 18 September 1959.

Decree Nisi for the dissolution of the Marriage, 17 September 1959

Divorce papers, John and Shirley Sangster. These include the following, with related documents including depositions by Shirley Sangster and affidavits.

Marriage Certificate, John Grant Sangster and Shirley Drew, 18 November 1949

Petition by Shirley Sangster for the Dissolution of Marriage, Sangster vs. Sangster, 4 February 1959; with related papers including depositions by Shirley Sangster and affidavits

Schnese, Petra. 2015. Personal communication to the author from Petra Schnese-Kleist-Sangster.

## Secondary Sources

Bebbington, Warren, ed. (1997), *The Oxford Companion to Australian Music*, Melbourne: Oxford University Press.

Bell, Graeme (1988), *Graeme Bell Australian Jazzman: His Autobiography*, Frenchs Forest NSW: Child & Associates Publishing Pty Ltd.

Bisset, Andrew (1987), *Black Roots White Flowers: A History of Jazz in Australia*, Sydney: ABC Enterprises. Note that the first edition was published in 1979. I have cited the second, revised, edition of 1987.

Clare, John, aka Gail Brennan (1995), *Bodgie Dada & The Cult of Cool*, Sydney: University of New South Wales Press.

Clare, John (2002), 'Review of The Last Will and Testament of John Sangster (1928-1955)', *MCA Music Forum* 8 (6), August/September: 45.

Commonwealth Reconstruction Training Scheme Administrative Records. Available online: https://www.naa.gov.au/sites/default/files/2020-05/fs-178-commonwealth-reconstruction-training-scheme-administrative-records.pdf (accessed 22 May 2023).

Dreyfus, Kay (1999), *Sweethearts of Rhythm: The Story of Australia's All-girl bands and Orchestras to the End of the Second World War*, Strawberry Hills NSW: Currency Press Pty Ltd.

Gould, Tony (2023), *A Ramble on Humour and Music With Occasional Diatribes Towards the Cloth-eared*, [Victoria]: Greenhill Publishing.

Hoban, Russell (1980), *Riddley Walker*, London: Picador.

Horne, Craig (2019), *Roots: How Melbourne Became the Live Music Capital of the World*, Melbourne: Melbourne Books.

Hughes, Dick (1977), *Daddy's Practising Again: An Australian Jazzman Looks Back and Around*, Richmond Victoria: Marlin Books

Hughes, Robert (1987), *The Fatal Shore: A History of the Transportation of Convicts to Australia 1787-1868*, London: Collins Harvill.

Jackson, Adrian and Andra Jackson (2022), *Wangaratta Festival of Jazz & Blues 30 Years*, Victoria: Melbourne Books.

Johnson, Bruce (1987), *The Oxford Companion to Australian Jazz*, Melbourne: Oxford University Press.

Johnson, Bruce (2023A), *Popular Music and Australian Culture: Across the Grain*, Newcastle upon Tyne: Cambridge Scholars Publishing.

Johnson, Bruce (2023B), '"The Frivolous, Scantily Clad 'Jazzing Flapper,' Irresponsible and Undisciplined": Jazz as a Feminine Domain', in James M. Reddan, Monika Herzig, and Michael Kahr (eds), *The Routledge Companion to Jazz and Gender*, New York and London: Routledge: 3–14.

Johnson, Bruce (2023C), *Earshot: Perspectives on Sound*, New York and London: Routledge.

Lee, Alan (1970), 'John Sangster', *Music Maker* (October): 11–13.

[Linehan, Norm, ed.] (1981), *Bob Barnard, Graeme Bell, Bill Haesler, John Sangster on The Australian Jazz Convention*, Sydney: The Australian Jazz Convention Trust Fund.

Mitchell, Jack (1988), *Australian Jazz on Record 1925-80*, Canberra: Australian Government Publishing Service.

Mitchell, Jack (1998), *More Australian Jazz on Record*, Canberra: National Film and Sound Archive; Jack Mitchell.

Mitchell, Jack (2002), *EMAJOR: Even More Australian Jazz on Record*. Melbourne: The Victorian Jazz Archive Inc.

Myers, Eric (1982), 'John Sangster: Music for Fluteman', *Jazz: the Australasian Contemporary Music Magazine*, December: 21.

Powell, Graeme, and Stuart MacIntyre (2015), *Land of Opportunity: Australia's Post-war Reconstruction*, Canberra: National Archives of Australia. Available online through naa.gov.au

Sandford Phil (2018), *The Lion Roars: The Musical Life of Willie 'The Lion' McIntyre*, Phil Sandford: No place given, but probably Melbourne.

Sangster, John (1988), *Seeing the Rafters: The Life and Times of an Australian Jazz Musician*, Ringwood Victoria: Penguin.

Sharpe, John ([2002]), *Don't Worry Baby. They'll Swing their Arses off: The Stories of Australian Jazz Musicians*, Australian Jazz Archive/Screensound Australia: Canberra.

Simmons, Adam (2023) 'Jazz in Melbourne', *Dingo: Australian Jazz Journal* 6 (Spring): 50–7.

Stevens, Timothy (2009), 'Early Ensembles and Recordings of John Grant Sangster', *Context: Journal of Music Research* 34: 35–42. Available online: http://search.informit.com.au/documentSummary;dn=729271157032915;res=IELHSS> ISSN: 1038-4006. Accessed 5/6/2015.

Stevens, Timothy (November 28, 2013), 'The Death of Isabella Dunn Sangster'. Available online: http://timstevens.com.au/the-death-of-isabella-dunn-sangster/. Accessed 5 June 2015.

Whiteoak, John, and Aline Scott-Maxwell (2003), *Currency Companion to Music and Dance in Australia*, Sydney: Currency Press.

Williams, Mike (1981), *The Australian Jazz Explosion*, Sydney: Angus & Robinson Publishers.

# Interviews

## *Chronological order*

**Each item, as cited in the text, begins in bold.**

**Gould and Lyall interview [2003]**. Interview by Martin Wright, transcribed by Timothy Stevens. Extracts from this interview are included on *The Lord of the Rings* CD reissue, Vol 2, CD 2, Move MD 3252, where the date is given as 19 January 2003.

**Len Barnard interview 2003**. Interview with Barnard, Len, 2003, on *The Lord of the Rings* CD reissue, Vol 2, CD 2, Move MD 3252. 19'47" minutes, 17 August. Interviewer not identified. I have added the first name in order to prevent confusion with his brother Bob, several times referred to in the text.

**Hounslow interview 2007**. Interview and transcription by Timothy Stevens. At 16/56 Beach Rd., Hampton, Victoria. 17 July.

**Gould interview 2007**. Interview and transcription by Timothy Stevens. At 5/59 Shelley St., Elwood Victoria. 4 August.

**Cosgrove interview 2009**. Bryony Cosgrove interview and transcription by Timothy Stevens 24 August.

# With John Sangster

**Bisset interview 1977**. John Sangster interview with Andrew Bisset, Sydney 27 August 1977, transcribed by Timothy Stevens.

**Linehan interview 1979**. John Sangster interview with Norman Linehan, 12 March 1979 transcribed by Timothy Stevens.

**Johnson interview 1988**. John Sangster interview with Bruce Johnson, Narrabeen around 1988 or 1989, transcribed by Timothy Stevens.

**Beilby interview 1994**. John Sangster interview with Roger Beilby, Montsalvat 28 January 1994 (?) transcribed by Timothy Stevens.

# Index


ABC (Australian Broadcasting
      Commission/
      Corporation)　41,
      46, 50
Aberdeen　35
Adams Tavern, Sydney　67
Adelaide　1, 2, 20, 33
*Ahead of Hair* (Recording)　51
Allawah Hotel, Sydney　46
Allen, Byron　80
'A moi de payer' (song)　103
'Among My Souvenirs' (song)　81
Ampersand (record Label)　29
Andrews Sisters, The　83
Ansell, Tony　71, 88, 89, 92
APRA (Australasian
      Performing Right
      Association)　50
Armstrong, Bill　22
Armstrong, Louis　79, 100
Armstrong, Warwick　28
Ashcroft, Johnny　47
*Australia and All That Jazz*
      (recordings)　51, 72
*Australian, The*
      (newspaper)　57

Australian Jazz Convention
      (AJC)　6, 11, 23, 32,
      33, 38, 39, 47
*Australian Jazz Quarterly*
      (magazine)　30
Australian Museum　72
Australian Record Awards　54
Ayler Albert　50, 79, 80

'Bag's Groove' (song)　101
Bailey, Judy　49, 55, 64
Ballarat　19, 20
Balliett, Whitney　83
Banks, Don　13
Banston, Jack　39
Barber, Chris　47
Barnard, Bob　52, 79, 85, 90,
      101, 109
Barnard, Len　21, 41, 52, 53,
      57, 58, 89, 95–100,
      111
Barr, Keith　68
Basie, Count　101, 107
Beatles, The　52
Bechet, Sidney　103
Beiderbecke, Bix　45, 90

Bell, Graeme    16, 21, 23, 25–8,
        30, 33, 36, 38–43,
        46–8, 54, 65, 79
Bell, Liz    42
Bell, Roger    12, 16, 21, 24, 26
Benge, Martin    54
Bennelong Hotel, Sydney    46
Bertles, Bob    102
'Best of Both Worlds' concert
        series, Sydney    50, 83
*Birth of the Blues, The*
        (movie)    18
Bloxsom, Ian    64
Blue Moon cabaret,
        Brisbane    41
'Bourbon Street Parade'
        (song)    99
Bray, Tich    17
Bridle, Sid    36
Brisbane    11, 17, 18, 44, 45, 57
Bromley, Sid    18
Brooks, Richard    92–3
Broonzy, Big Bill    40
Brown, Brian    23, 67
Buchanan, Tony    101, 104, 106
Buddle, Errol    17, 105
Burrows, Don    17, 49–51, 56,
        64, 66, 69, 71, 73, 75,
        79, 80, 90, 107
Byrnes, George    45
Byrnes, Janice Patricia, aka Bo
        Diddley qv    45, 56

Byrnes, Jesse, *née*
        Wakeham    45

Caloundra, Queensland    46
Canberra    19
Carroll, Lewis    63
Carson, Ron    50
Cavalcade of Jazz (concert)    22
Celebrity Club, Brisbane    41
Cell Block Theatre
        (Sydney)    50, 83
'Charleston' (song)    105
Christie, Lyn    49, 82
Clare, John    50, 68
Commodore Records    26
Commonwealth Employment
        Service    13
Commonwealth
        Reconstruction
        Training Scheme    13
'Conjur-Man' (song)    50
Contemporary Art Society    26
Cooper, Bert    26
Cosgrove, Bryony    21
Coughlan, Frank    26, 49
Crossfire (band)    56, 83
Cutler, Sir Rohan    75

*Daily Mirror, The* (Sydney
        newspaper)    47
Dallwitz, Dave    33, 52
Dankworth, Johnny    40

'Danny Boy' (song)    81

Dargie, Horrie    47

Davidson, Jim    20

Davies, Bill 'Spadge'    16

Department of Post War
Reconstruction    12

Diddley, Bo 45, 56; *see also*
Byrnes, Janice Patricia

'Diminuendo and Crescendo in
Blue' (song)    102

*Dingo* magazine    23

Donegan, Lonnie    47

Dorsey, Tom[my]    83

*Downbeat* magazine    18

Drew, Shirley    30, 39

Dukas, Paul    103

Durham, Judy    25

Dyer, Warwick (Wocka)    31, 38


Eliot, T.S.    103

Ellington, Duke    30, 47, 52, 73,
80, 83, 86, 89, 90, 102,
107

El Rocco, jazz venue Sydney    3,
45, 49, 50, 64, 66, 84,
85, 87, 91, 105

Eltham, Victoria    26, 67

Eureka Hot Jazz Society    28

Eureka Youth League    26, 28, 33

'Exactly Like You' (song)    102

Expo 67, Montreal    51, 80, 81

Expo 70, Japan    51, 64, 67

Fawkner Park Kiosk,
Melbourne    18, 26

*Fawlty Towers* (TV series)    100

Featherstone, Benny    26

'Flowers for Elizabeth' (song)    57

*Fluteman* (recording)    56

*Fluteman, The* (movie)    56

*For Leon Bismark*
(recording)    52, 90

Forsyth, Cecil    52

'Freight Train' (song)    47

*Funky Phantom, The* (animated
TV series)    53


Gabler, Milt    26

Gamelan orchestra    64

Garcia, Russell    52, 81

Golla, George    50–2

Gonsalves, Paul    102

Goodman, Benny    18, 22

Gough, Dorothy (later
Bell)    42, 43

Gould, Tony    3, 23, 55, 63, 66,
69, 71–5, 78, 79, 81,
88–95, 111

Gowans, Brad    27

Graham, Kenny    40

Grainger, Percy    81


Haesler, Bill    1

*Hair* (stage musical)    51, 64

Handy, John    80

Harris, Max   26

'Heide' group (artists)   26

Helpmann, Robert   67

Herron, Ken   67

Hindemith, Paul   52

Hoban, Russel   63

Hobart   20, 33

*Hobbit Suite, The*   4, 54, 64,
          65, 85

*Hollywood Hotel* (movie)   18

Hounslow, Keith   18, 23, 30,
          32, 33, 70, 71, 75, 76

Hughes, Dick   2, 11, 16, 24, 29

Hughes, Michael   45


Ingram, Ken   13

*In the Wild with Harry Butler* (TV
          series)   52, 72

*It Don't Mean a Thing if it Ain't
          Got that Doo-Wup
          Doo-Wup Doo-Wup*
          (recording)   55

'It Don't Mean A Thing If It
          Ain't Got That Swing'
          (song)   47

Ives, Charles   81

'I wish I could shimmy like
          my Sister Kate'
          (song)   102, 109


Jackson, Milt   101

Jackson, Peter   4

James, Bob   50

James, Harry   83

Japan   41, 44, 51; *see also* Expo
          70

*Jazz Australia* (recording)   50

*Jazz Night* (radio
          programme   3UZ);
          later *Swing Night*   29

*Jazz Notes* (magazine)   30, 33

Johnson, Frank   21, 28

Jones, Kevin   57

Jupp, Eric   48


'Kaffir Song' (song)   50

Kaiser, Kathleen Margaret
          Therese Anne
          (Peggy)   42–5

Kaminsky, Max   12, 27, 29

Keane, Larry   26

Kenny, Mick   83

'King of the Zulus' (song)   99

'Kisses Sweeter than Wine'
          (song)   47

Kitchen, Geoff   52

Koffman, Moe   108

Korea   41


*Landscapes of Middle Earth*
          (recording)   4, 54

*Last Will and Testament of John
          Sangster (1928–1955),
          The* (recording)   57, 58

Launceston   20

Lear, Edward   55, 63, 91, 92, 94

Lee, Alan   23, 52, 67, 69

Lennon, John   63

Leonard's Cabaret
      Melbourne   27

Libaek, Sven   52, 68

Lichine, David   81

Liepolt, Horst   16

Limb, Bobby   53

Liszt, Franz   103

'Little Rock Getaway'
      (song)   102

Logan, Giuseppe   80

London   1, 22

*Lord of the Rings* Suite   52–5,
      58, 64, 65, 76, 81–3,
      85, 86, 95–111
    Hobbits   1, 4, 6, 52, 54, 64,
      65, 71, 85
    individual songs from the
      suite
      'Ants and
        Entwives'   108, 109
      'Arwen's Regret'   102
      'The Balrog'   101
      'Beware the
        Barrow-Wight'   101
      'Bilbo's Birthday
        Party'   100
      'Blues for Boromir'   108
      'Blues for Denethor'   100

'Celeborn Celbrant'   105

'Eleventy-One
      Today'   107

'Elvish Dance'   100

'Elvish Tea-Party with
      Dance'   100

'Encore Gandalph'   105

'Fair Eowyn'   107

'Farewell Lothrian'   103

'Frodo's Fantasy'   103

'Gandalph the
      White'   107

'Gladriel'   106

'The Glittering
      Caves'   107

'Goldberry'   105

'Goodnight'   97

'The Great Battle'   86, 98

'The Grey Havens' [aka 'The
      Grey Heavens']   108

'Hairy Foolish Shoeless
      Feet'   106

'Hoblyti-Hoblyta'   105

'Ithildin'   102

'Legolas: Elf'   103

'Longbottom Leaf'   97

'Lullaby in Lorien'   107

'Merry-go-round'   104

'The Mirror of
      Galadriel'   106

'The Misty
      Mountains'   107

'Nazgul'   104

'Off to Adventures'   107

'The O'Goblin Tattoo'   99

'Oliphants'   102

'Orcs'   104

'Phantasmagoria for
    Moria'   104

'Proper Fourteen-
    Twenty'   108

'The Ride of the
    Rohirrim'   107

'Ringbearer'   100, 104

'Rivendell Rort'   102

'Sam the Man'   107

'Shelob's Lair'   104

'Three Cheers for
    Smeagol'   106

'Three is Company'   100

'The Sweetness and
    Light Rag'   100

'Thank You
    Perfessor'   102

'Tom Bombadil'   99

'The Uruk-Hai'   101

'Vale Theoden'   102, 109

'V-M-E Day (a Mondorian
    Phantasmagoria)'
    98

Orcs   4, 6, 71, 104

'Love Walked in' (song)   81

Lyall, Graham   54, 64, 66, 74, 87,
    91, 95, 107, 108, 111

Lyttelton, Humphrey   40

McCarthy, John   55, 85, 101,
    109–10

McIntyre, Will   22

McIvor, Bob   90, 101, 102, 109

Maddison, Neville   26

*Magic of Music,* The (TV
    programme)   48

Mahler, Gustave   81

'Making Whoopee' (song)   102

Mancini, Henry   52, 81

Marginson, Ray   29

*Marinetti* (film)   51

Meadmore, Clem   42

'Mean to Me' (song)   102

*Meditation* (recording)   55, 86

Melbourne   1, 5, 11, 13–15,
    18–30, 32, 35, 36, 38,
    41, 42, 44, 45, 52, 78

Melbourne, University of   13, 24

Melbourne
    Conservatorium   14

*Melbourne Sun*, the   24

Melbourne Technical
    School   34–5

Mick Moylan's (pub,
    Sydney)   48

Miller, Bill   15, 18, 29–30

Milligan, Spike   63

Mills Brothers, The   83

Mitchell, Jack   7

Mitchell Library, The
    (Sydney)  8, 41, 43
Mole, Miff  90
Monsbourgh, Ade  16, 24, 26, 27, 33, 47
Montsalvat Jazz Festival  58, 81
'Mooche, The' (song)  47, 90
'Moonglow' (song)  102
Morton, Ferdinand 'Jelly Roll'  82, 97
*Movietone* (newseels)  18
Munro, Charlie  79
Murphy, Russ  27, 39
Murray, Sonny  80
*Music Maker* (magazine)  30
Myer Music Bowl  78

*Naked City, The* (TV series)  108
Narrabeen, Sydney  4, 53, 57, 66, 68, 74, 86, 87
Nepean Hotel, Portsea  27
Newport Jazz Festival  102
Newstead, Tony  13, 21, 24, 38
New Sydney Woodwind Quintet  50
New Theatre, The, Melbourne  38
'New Woman', The  14
New York  22, 26, 80
Niven, David  68
'Nobody's Sweetheart Now' (song)  90

Nolan, Col  1, 49, 51, 52, 67, 68
Nolan, Sidney  26
Noosa Jazz Party  57
Nutwood Rug (band)  51
'Oh That Sign' (song)  29

Old Push, The (Sydney jazz venue)  55
Oliver, Joe 'King'  99

Partch, Harry  63
*Peaceful* (recording)  55, 86
Pearce, Ian  14
Percussion Society of Australia  63
'Perdido' (song)  102
Perth (Australia)  18, 25, 33
Perth (Scotland)  35, 37
'Pilgrimage for Pop' festival  51
Port Jackson Jazz Band  21, 48
Port Moresby, New Guinea  18
Portsea Four (band)  27
'Potato Head Blues' (song, recording)  79
Powerhouse, The (jazz venue Melbourne)  22
Price, Ray  1, 2, 48, 49, 67, 79
Princess Alexandra  48
Pringle, James  35
'Pub With No Beer, The' (song)  47

Qua, Chris   74, 90
'Rain on Water' (song)   50, 79

Ravel, Maurice   52, 81, 89
Ray, Johnny   47
Re-establishment and
        Employment Act of
        1945   12–13
Regal Zonophone record
        label   28, 36
*Requiem (for a loved one)*
        (recording)   37,
        45, 56
Riddle, Nelson   108
*Riddley Walker* (novel)   63
Riverside Jazz Band   21, 38
Roberts, Don 'Pixie'   27
Rock Island Line' (song)   47
Rohde, Bryce   17
Rose, Pat   1, 3, 67
Royal Australian Navy
        Band   74
'Sally' (song)   81

Sangster, Isabella Dunn (*née*
        Davidson)   35, 37
Sangster, John   1–8, 11, 16, 17,
        22, 23, 25, 27, 28, 48–9,
        53, 55–7; *see also Lord
        of the Rings* suite
    Alan Watson 'party'   30–1,
        33, 39

alcohol   73–6, 90–2
Australian identity   72–3
compositions and
        compositional
        and recording
        methods   70–1, 73,
        85–97
death   57–8
death of mother   37
early life   35–7
early performances   33, 36,
        38, 39
eccentricity   65–70
El Rocco period   49–50
Graeme Bell
        association   39–42,
        45–8
international tours   50,
        51, 64
progressive, fusion and
        experimental
        developments   50,
        51, 56, 64, 79–80
sensibility and
        aesthetics   61–85
sonocentricity,
        sonophilia   62–5
studio, film and TV
        work   52, 53
Sangster, John Sr.   35
Santamaria, Mongo   80
Saratsina   75

Saul's Coffee Lounge
(Melbourne)  27
Schäuble, Niko  23
Schnese, Petra, aka Petra
Schnese-Kleist-
Sangster  57, 58,
76, 79
Scots College Melbourne  16
Seekers, The (band)  25
Shaw, Artie  12
Shepp, Archie  80
Sherburn, Nevill  54
Shop Swingers, The (band)  24
Silbereisen, Lou  27, 39
Silker, George  26
Simmons, Adam  23, 25
Skiffle  47
Smith, Howie  72, 73
'Snake Rag' (song)  100
*Sorcerer's Apprentice, The*  103
Soup Plus (Jazz venue
Sydney)  110
Southern Jazz Group, The
(band)  38
*Spiritual Unity* (recording)  79
Stage Door, The (jazz venue
Melbourne)  27
Stein, Harry  28, 33
Stevens, Timothy  21, 30, 35, 39
Stewart, Rex  30
Stockhausen, Karlheinz  81
Stravinsky, Igor  52, 81, 103

Sullivan, Joe  102
*Sun, The* (Sydney newspaper)
47
Sun Ra  50, 80, 82
'Swinging Shepherd Blues'
(song)  108
*Swing Night; see Jazz Night*
Sydney  1, 2, 17, 19–21, 23, 28,
33, 41–3, 45–8, 50,
51, 55
Sydney Conservatorium of
Music  73
*Sydney Morning Herald,
The* (Sydney
newspaper)  22
Sydney String Quartet  81
Sydney Symphony
Orchestra  50
Sylvania Hotel, Sydney  48

Tack, George  13, 21, 24, 38
Taperell, Chris  55
Taylor, Cecil  50, 80
Teagarden, Jack  18
*Tempo* magazine  18, 30
Thompson, George  84
Thompson, Laurie  55, 111
Thoms, Albie  51
*Three Strings and a Dash*
(recording)  79
Tokyo  22
Tolkien, J.R.R.  4, 54

Tough, Bob   26
Tough, Dave   90
*Trad Dad* (TV show)   48
Tully (band)   51
Turner, C. Ian   33

Ubu group   51
Underhill, Tony   28
Universal Training Scheme,
        The   28
*Untouchables, The* (TV
        series)   108
Uptown Club, The   28, 37
*Uttered Nonsense (The Owl
        and the Pussycat)*
        (recording)   55,
        63, 92

Vaughan, Sarah   50
Velvet Tavern, The Adelaide jazz
        venue   1
Vermont Scout Troop   36
Victorian Jazz Lovers'
        Society   27

Waks, Nathan   62, 81, 109
Walker, Mickey   26
Waller, Fats   82
Wangaratta Jazz and Blues
        Festival   57
Wanliss, Tom   22
Warne, Alf   26
Washboard Rhythm Kings   18
Watson, Alan   27, 30, 31, 39, 49
Westlake, Donald   50
'[When we Danced at
        the] Mardi Gras'
        (song)   102
Wilson, Dennis   100
World War Two   5, 11, 12, 14,
        15, 17, 20, 29
Wright, Judith   62
Wright, Mark   58

Xenakis, Iannis   81

Young, Bob 'Beetles'   52
'You Ought to be in Pictures'
        (song)   102